W9-ARB-116

The Japanese Challenge to U.S. Industry

The Japanese Challenge to U.S. Industry

Jack Baranson
Developing World Industry and
Technology, Inc.

LexingtonBooks
D.C. Heath and Company
Lexington, Massachusetts
Toronto

This book is based in part on work conducted under contract for the Office of Technology Assessment (OTA) of the United States Congress intended to provide background material for an OTA assessment. The information presented and the views expressed in this book are those of the author and not necessarily those of OTA.

Library of Congress Cataloging in Publication Data

Baranson, Jack.
The Japanese challenge to U.S. industry.

Bibliography: p.
Includes index.
1. Japanese—Industries. 2. United States Industries. 3. Japan—
Commerce—United States. 4. United States—Commerce—Japan. I. Title.
HC462.9.B36   338.0952   80-8889
ISBN 0-669-04402-4   AACR2

Copyright © 1981 by D.C. Heath and Company

Second printing, May 1982

Published simultaneously in Canada

Printed in the United States of America

International Standard Book Number: 0-669-04402-4

Library of Congress Catalog Card Number: 80-8889

Contents

Contents

List of Tables

Foreword

This book is highly relevant to the fundamental economic-policy rethinking that the United States is undergoing in the early 1980s. It examines Japan's remarkable successes in global competition to see what can be learned for U.S. policy and business practice. Its lessons go far beyond questions of trade competitiveness to emphasize the vital importance of long-range planning, technological vision, and risk taking in the Japanese system. Repeatedly it contrasts the U.S. executive's focus on quarterly-earnings reports with the Japanese managerial team's primary focus on long-range development of the product, the market, and the methods of production.

The extraordinary achievements of Japan in world competition, and especially Japan's formidable pace in catching up with and surpassing U.S. and European enterprises technologically, have given rise to many explanations. The most popular is that this performance results from Japanese government subsidies and trade barriers and unfair Japanese trade practices abroad. This explanation is very convenient since it puts the blame for the United States' lagging competitiveness on others. It may seem far better to blame the Japanese for unfair competition than to blame one's own industry for flawed performance. This theory has diverted policy-makers and industrial managers from serious analysis of what is wrong with our own system and of what we can learn from successes elsewhere. In this book, Dr. Baranson, whose recognized expertise in the role of technological change in international business activity is unequaled, has tried to throw some light on the nature of the Japanese challenge and on U.S. responses.

Baranson sets aside many myths about Japan. For example, the dependence of Japan's economy on trade is far less than that of many other nations (such as the United Kingdom, France, Britain, West Germany, and Canada). Where Japan has been accused of giving primacy to exports, the reality is that the Japanese domestic market traditionally has absorbed the lion's share of production of key export products. Every major Japanese export industry, he points out, has achieved significant overseas penetration only after a large domestic market base had emerged. As for the alleged role of government aid to industry in Japan, he notes that direct government subsidies or financial assistance to any given industry are difficult to detect and appear to be modest at most.

What then is the magic formula? The forward view of Japanese industry—to envision what will be needed and how to make it in volume, cheaply—is a starting point. In Japan, Baranson believes, there is a clear recognition that comparative advantage of industries is a dynamic rather than a fixed process and that it is directly related to technological development. He concludes that "the ability to manage technological change in a dynamic world economy may well be the decisive competitive advantage in world trade.''

What is it that facilitates exploitation of technological change? First, a highly educated working force is important. Japan's literacy rate is an astounding 99.8 percent. The percentage of the population completing Japanese secondary school, which has higher standards than do U.S. schools, is far greater than even Japan's closest educational rivals, Canada and the United States. Second, such people should be effectively utilized. The ratio of design and engineering staff to the work force in Japan's industrial enterprises is often four or five times that of the United States.

In Japan, there is a continuous emphasis on rationalization and modernization of the production system as well as the product, with extraordinary emphasis on both quality control and cost-effectiveness and on extending the capabilities of workers by increased automation. Capital spending, based on a higher savings level and lower personal taxes and on an economic and financial environment that is conductive to risk taking, is sufficient not only to maintain but to advance technological capabilities and relative competitive position.

And where, then, does the government come in? What is the nature of this phenomenon we have come to call Japan, Inc.? Baranson argues that the government-industry relationship is much more cooperative than in the United States and that government is far more supportive of industry efforts. But that support is not so much tangible as it is a way of thinking and guiding. The government, working with industry, identifies key areas of technological promise, and private commercial banks then give greater emphasis to these areas, in the comfortable knowledge that the tax system rewards risk taking and that the areas identified have a good chance for success. The government often encourages industrial cooperation and exchange of information among companies, especially in advanced-technology areas. If the companies in these high-risk areas begin to get into trouble through duplication of effort, the government may encourage mergers or more formal joint ventures. Economic concentration policy and antitrust policy are carried out in a global context; it is believed that to compete by world standards may require fewer, not more, firms at home.

The United States has been a model of entirely opposite policies: discourage cooperation among firms, encourage duplication, discourage mergers, treat large U.S. firms as if the marketplace is defined by our national borders, and consider any increase in relative size as leading in a bad direction. Dr. Baranson concludes about the United States that ''a reevaluation of antitrust regulations and other factors fostering inefficient, self-defeating adversary relationships in American industry is clearly necessary.'' This book thus shows that there are lessons to be learned from Japanese experience, lessons that are relevant to the U.S. economy.

Since the American rate of capital investment began to slip in the late 1960s, and especially during the slow-growth period of the 1970s, I have thought that a liberal trade policy and a liberal market economy would be difficult to maintain. We live at a time when growth of trade, capital flows, and communications have made the U.S. economy far more interactive with the rest of the world than in previous decades. We face the emergence of many new international competitors from the developing world as well as Japan's rapid advances in higher technology. We have to deal with energy disruptions, commodity and currency turbulence, and inflation. Our industrial competitiveness and our relative economic strength must inexorably diminish unless we can restructure the economy to deal with the new realities. But to restructure, to improve our economic base to meet and beat our competitors, we have to grow much faster and set aside a far larger share of our growth for future development of our economy—in the form of greatly increased capital spending and larger expenditures on research and development. Although the new realities call for accelerated adjustment of our capital and technological base, we have instead slowed down.

The new economic policies proposed by the Reagan administration may correct this loss of drive and confidence in the future. Much of the Japanese experience in dealing with and mastering the commercial development of technology should be drawn on in the development of our own economy; however, even this is not enough. We will also need to change our management culture, to emphasize strategic planning and long-range performance, and to deemphasize quarterly earnings and short-term cost and cash management. That is a tall order, but the Japanese industrial complex has no monopoly on long-range vision. A method of planning and decision making that is focused on the future and based on a system that rewards risk gives Japanese management its remarkable record of success.

The new U.S. economic policies may create an environment that will encourage a similar kind of management orientation in this country. But management culture does not change quickly, built as it is on bureaucracies that are just as rigid and resistant to change as government bureaucracies—sometimes even more so.

Dr. Baranson suggests that we forget the question of blame for past irritations and failures and instead face forward, anticipating tomorrow's marketplace with a technological capability geared to it. As we look forward, we should bear in mind Japan's lesson that competitiveness is a dynamic process, based on mastering technology rather than being overtaken by it.

Harald B. Malmgren
Malmgren, Inc.
Washington, D.C.

Preface and Acknowledgments

During the past decade, a broad spectrum of Japanese industries has developed into formidable international competition in high technology. Export markets are of critical importance to Japanese firms in their overall corporate strategies, and the U.S. market is the most important. As a consequence, a wide range of U.S. industries, including highly visible ones such as the automotive and electronics industries, has had to face growing Japanese competitiveness in these areas and has suffered as a consequence.

The true nature of the Japanese commercial threat has been imperfectly understood in the United States. The economic dislocation that Japanese competitors have inflicted on their U.S. counterparts and the calculated efficiency with which the Japanese have been successfully assaulting international markets have served to distort an accurate perception of the Japanese industrial phenomenon. A common image of the Japanese threat is one of ungrateful, insensitive, and rapacious Japanese businessmen engaged in unfair trading practices, aided and abetted by the Japanese government. U.S. firms that seek to portray the Japanese menace as a prime cause of their worsening commercial prospects and then call for protectionist measures are doing themselves and the nation a disservice. The tendency of many U.S. firms to try to meet the Japanese commercial challenge anywhere other than the marketplace (including protracted litigation) only delays much-needed rethinking of long-range corporate policy.

The goal of this book is to provide deeper insights into the Japanese industrial phenomenon by focusing on a major segment of the consumer electronics industry. The patterns that occur in that sector are now being reflected in other industrial sectors, including, most recently, automobile products. Although some Japanese firms may have engaged to some extent in what their business adversaries would term unfair business practices, it is dangerously misleading to view these practices as major causes of Japanese success, when that success is much more the result of legitimate, discerning, farsighted corporate policies and practices. A clearer perception by the U.S. audience of how the Japanese do business should serve two crucial purposes: to contribute to a better relationship with one of our most important allies and to present to the U.S. business community a commercial model that deserves emulation, particularly in terms of industrial management and longer-range corporate planning.

Acknowledgments

This book is an outgrowth of contract research on the Japanese and American color-television and videotape-recorder industries (for the U.S. Congress's Office of Technology Assessment and the Office of Science and Technology of the U.S. Department of Commerce), and on the Japanese automobile industry (for the Federal Trade Commission). The material presented in the book is based upon fieldwork I carried out in Japan and in the United States in the fall of 1977 and in the spring of 1980, as well as on several hundred articles, documents, and books that I reviewed in connection with the past studies. A selected bibliography of these source materials appears at the end of the book.

I am indebted to Richard Dana, the principal research associate in the earlier studies, who was responsible for developing a large portion of the material in the book. I am also especially grateful to Yoshi Tsurumi (Baruch College), Harald Malmgren (Malmgren, Inc.), and Chris Kristoff (General Motors) for reviewing the original manuscript and for several insights that I have incorporated and noted where appropriate.

Part I
Sources of Japanese Competitiveness

1 Overview

Until the late 1960s U.S. industry enjoyed a technological preeminence and a related market dominance in a wide range of industrial and commercial products. During the past decade, however, the competitive challenge of Japanese industry has intensified, beginning in world markets and now making substantial inroads into the U.S. market itself. The consumer electronics industry provides a vivid example. In this industry these inroads into the U.S. market began with less-sophisticated consumer electronic products and eventually spread to advanced-generation products such as videotape recording. Videotape recording was invented in the United States, but its commercialization has been completely taken over by Japanese firms. This sophisticated equipment is now manufactured in Japan and supplied to U.S. consumer electronics firms for marketing in the United States under their brand names.

Successful market penetration by Japanese enterprise has now spread to traditional areas of U.S. competitive strength, such as the automobile and business-machine industries. There are already indications of significant advances into current areas of U.S. strength in the microprocessor, computer, and aircraft equipment fields. The controversy over the competitiveness of Japanese-based industry in the U.S. economy has intensified as the U.S. trade position has deteriorated and as industrial employment has eroded.

Opinions have varied widely on the underlying causes of the meteoric rise of Japanese industry and the corresponding decline of segments of U.S. industry. There have been allegations that Japanese industry engages in unfair trade practices and takes collusive action with its government to favor Japanese enterprise and to discriminate against foreign companies; other strong accusations charge that Japan undertakes industrial espionage to steal our technological secrets. Japanese competition has led more to a protectionist reaction in America than to an assessment of the causes of our apparent loss of the technological dynamics that have maintained U.S. competitiveness in the world economy in the past.[1]

The evidence presented in this book indicates that the competitive structure and dynamics of the Japanese economy and Japanese enterprise vis-à-vis those of the United States constitute the real underlying causes of the Japanese challenge. A number of factors contribute to Japanese competitive strength:

3

1. The progressive ability of Japanese industry to design and engineer in-
    dustrial products and production systems and to manage them effec-
    tively at successive stages of growth.
2. The quality and productivity of its labor force, reinforced by effective
    organization and management attuned to Japanese culture and society.
3. The continuing rationalization and modernization of plant and equip-
    ment, including mounting investments in automation and persistent
    concern with cost-effectiveness and meticulous quality control.
4. An economic and financial environment conducive to risk taking and
    that supplies the capital resources necessary to maintain and advance
    technological capabilities.
5. Government-industry relations that are highly supportive of Japanese
    enterprise and its competitive position in world trade (in contrast to the
    adversary position that often characterizes U.S. government-industry
    relations).

The Japanese consumer electronics industry is characterized by an integrated structural relationship between the larger end-product companies
and the thousands of medium- to small-size firms that supply them. The industry has an ability to maintain a broad spectrum of products (in a variety
of configurations for segments of different world markets) in the face of intense competition, while remaining cost-effective. It is aggressive in
marketing on a global basis and responds to special tastes and demands of
segments of the world market. Its symbiotic relationships with adjacent industries provide critical componentry at a cost and quality that enhance
end-product competitiveness from the standpoint of both unit costs and at-
tractiveness to consumers. Finally, the industry can quickly and efficiently
mobilize its financial resources and provide cost-effective organization and
management of production facilities at home and abroad.

The Japanese experience demonstrates a fundamental trend in the world
economy: the growing role of technology in shaping the dynamics of
shifting comparative advantage in world trade. It also reinforces Adam
Smith's timeless observation that the ultimate wealth of nations lies in the
knowledge and skills of its people and in their ability to organize and apply
knowledge and use and develop human resources effectively. A basic difference between U.S. and Japanese strategies in managing global systems is
that U.S. firms delay in the needed commitment of capital to research and
development (R&D), manpower, and production upgrading, whereas Japanese firms invest with much less hesitation in their human and technology
resources and in automated facilities in order to reduce costs, design out
quality-control problems, and develop new markets.

The typical response patterns of U.S. and Japanese firms to intensified
competition stand in marked contrast. In the early 1970s Japanese con-

sumer electronics firms began redesigning television sets for more-efficient production and automated their plants to increase export volumes and thereby reduce unit production costs. The impressive productivity gains by these firms have permitted them to absorb most of the increase in export prices resulting from the appreciating yen. The typical American response to the challenge of Japanese imports has been to freeze product designs and to export existing production technologies to low-wage areas as a cost-reduction measure. In contrast to the persistent and aggressive techno-logical advance of Japanese enterprise, U.S. firms have been reducing R&D expenditures, moving U.S. production facilities offshore, or phasing out high-technology product lines in favor of lower-risk profit centers.

Some analysts have become optimistic about the recovery of U.S. in-dustry strength based on the flow of investments into the United States by, for example, Japanese consumer electronics and automobile equipment assemblers. But we believe that this will simply enable Japanese firms to bypass rising U.S. protectionism more effectively while strengthening their technological capabilities at our expense. In consumer electronics, the U.S. economy will supply low-skill labor for the assembly of a limited range of components, while sophisticated products will continue to be imported from Japan. An even more far-reaching result will be the further enhance-ment of Japanese design engineering capabilities at the expense of those of the United States.

It is essential to the growth and performance of the U.S. economy that it adapt more rapidly and more effectively to economic and technical change in the world economy, and particularly in regard to the Japanese challenge. There is an urgent need to create new incentives for U.S. enter-prise to invest in technological change to keep pace with the high-wage U.S. economy. Our evidence indicates that U.S. firms have contributed as much to the decline of U.S. competitiveness as have the foreign "devils."

U.S. enterprise and related financial and labor management support structures have largely failed to pursue and accept the technological change and adjustment that is so vital to competitiveness in today's world economy. The larger U.S. corporations increasingly have become averse to the risk taking associated with dynamic technical change, and corporate management has shown a clear tendency to move toward the easier profit centers, failing to develop new product generations and prematurely relin-quishing market shares in established lines to Japanese competition.

Most U.S. firms also seem to lack the determination to develop and sus-tain global marketing strategies on anything like the scale demonstrated by their Japanese counterparts. All this is occurring at a stage of world in-dustrial development where U.S. industry must increase its rate of invest-ment in automation (and related product-design changes) if it is to meet the built-in advantages of the Japanese industrial base. U.S. firms are also taking an increasingly parochial view, failing to seize upon timely opportunities to penetrate world markets at a time when such action could counteract foreign competition.

Conversely a few American firms have responded to the Japanese challenge by beating the Japanese at their own game. One such company is Texas Instruments (TI), which resembles a Japanese company in many respects and, significantly, is one of the few U.S. firms with successful manufacturing operations and design engineering facilities in Japan. Like Japanese companies, TI stresses a strong work ethic, competitive zeal, loyalty to the company, and carefully planned, rational decision making. The company has a strong commitment to technological innovation and aggressive pursuit of market shares, backed by sustained investments in R&D and new plants and equipment. Sustained expenditures for improvements in product design and manufacturing methods ensure rapid movement down the learning curve. (The *learning curve* is an analytical management tool used to plot an enterprise's decreases in unit production cost, or increases in production efficiency, as a function of increased volume of production. The steeper the slope of the curve, the faster the learning of how to decrease costs and increase efficiency through production expansion. Japanese firms in a wide range of industries have made use of the learning curve principle.) The firm's market strategy is designed to achieve volume in order to reduce costs. TI is one of the few American companies that has penetrated the Japanese market.

On a more pessimistic note, the Japanese challenge is extending itself across a broader spectrum of industries. Many of the same corporate strategies that have proven so successful for Japanese consumer electronics firms are also reaping rewards for other segments of Japanese industry. For example, Japanese firms have been making a successful assault on the business copier market in the United States by using these strategies. Having already captured virtually the whole lower segment of this market (which was left undeveloped by the U.S. industry), the Japanese are aggressively designing and marketing higher-range copiers at the expense of the U.S. industry. Robotics is another major industry in which Japan has taken a strong lead, accounting for nearly half of the world's installed robots.[2] The major sources of competitiveness for these industries lie in a strong dedication to increasingly automated high-volume production, aggressive export strategies calling for initial penetration of the low-priced range of a foreign market and gradual movement into higher-priced market segments, and a commitment to invest heavily in the upgrading of technology and production capabilities from a long-term perspective.

We hope that this book will provide some new and revealing perspectives on the nature of the Japanese industrial challenge and lead to more-perceptive and realistic prescriptive measures than has been the case so far.

Accusations of unfair trade practices and progressive protectionism as a paradigm of diagnosis and prescription can only exacerbate our economic predicament. If we are to compete in the world economy, we must face up to the realities of intensified competition from Japanese and other sources and realize that our economic salvation lies in greater efficiency and effectiveness in industrial management, coupled with discerning and cooperative government policies.

Notes

1. An interesting parallel of a siege economy has emerged in England. See "The Cambridge Protectionists," *Wall Street Journal*, 24 April 1978.

2. See "Business Brief: Japan's Gentle Persuaders," *Economist*, January 17, 1981. See also report by Daiwa Securities America (One Liberty Plaza, New York, N.Y. 10006) on "Robotics in Japan," 3 July 1980.

2 Structural Underpinnings

Japan's postwar economy has been one of the largest and fastest growing in the world. Its gross national product for 1980 of over $1 trillion was surpassed only by the United States and the Soviet Union. During the 1960s, the country's assessed rate of economic growth was more than double that of the United States (an 11.4 percent average for Japan as compared to 4.2 percent for the United States). The sustained expansion of industrial exports has been a major contribution to economic growth and advancing productivity in Japan. Japanese emphasis upon exports stems in part from the necessity to pay for indispensable imports of raw material, energy, capital equipment, and technology but also reflects a national approach to economic efficiency through volume production for world markets. For some time Japan's exports have been highly sophisticated, technology-intensive manufactured products. The high quality of its early optical goods and motorcycles rapidly altered American perceptions of Japan in the 1950s as a maker of silk, pottery, cheap toys, and souvenirs. Today there is a growing demand in the United States for Japanese-made cars, steel, machine tools, office equipment, and a wide variety of home entertainment products, to name but a few of the country's major exports.

Japan's constant drive to expand exports has contributed to production efficiencies. Expanded production volumes have permitted Japanese firms to move down the learning curve, thereby reducing unit costs and allowing them to accumulate production experience more rapidly and improve their competitive position against foreign firms at home and abroad.

Entry into world markets has also exposed even the larger oligopolistic Japanese firms to the discipline of price and quality competition in these markets and thus indirectly contributed to their success. This discipline has been transmitted to the myriad of domestic supplier industries not directly participating in international trade. Japanese firms have consciously adapted quality as the key strategic variable in penetrating and, more importantly, retaining both domestic and world markets. Unlike American firms, Japanese firms have refused to trade off quality for productivity. Their dual concern has been to mass produce on a cost-effective basis and to improve product quality.

The expansion of markets in dynamic and high-productivity industries also has made it easier for the Japanese economy to phase out low-performing sectors. The domestic market, however, has absorbed the lion's share of Japan's production. Indeed Japan's dependence on exports, though greater than that of the United States, is less than that of many other industrialized nations. In 1979 the country exported only 12.6 percent of GNP, while German, British, and French exports averaged twice this percentage. Every major Japanese export industry has achieved significant overseas penetration only after a large domestic market base had emerged. Japanese color television, for example, caught on domestically in 1964, but significant export did not materialize until 1969. Similarly penetration of the U.S. automobile market did not occur until some time after the sustained growth of the domestic auto market.

Cultural and Historical Background

Various factors underlie Japan's economic success in the postwar period. Several elements in Japan's cultural and historical background help to explain its current achievements. The character of the Japanese people has been a major element in Japan's rapid industrialization and economic growth. The qualities and traits often associated with the Protestant ethic—frugality and a preparedness to work hard and postpone consumption by saving and investment—are clearly evident in the culture and tradition of the people. The propensity to save and invest in future growth is strong on both the individual and corporate levels. The rate of personal income savings has consistently been higher in Japan than in the United States or Western Europe and currently is about 22 percent of disposable income, as compared to 15 percent in conservative West Germany and a meager 5 percent in the United States. Individual Japanese usually deposit their savings in city banks and commercial banks, which in turn channel funds into investment loans to business. It has been estimated that Japanese industry, particularly heavy chemicals and durable goods, generates roughly half of its growth rate from this source, as opposed to the Western method of selling public stock or issuing bonds.

Japanese frugality stems in part from the country's resource-poor nature but is also reinforced by preferential taxes on savings deposits. Relatively low rates of inflation make savings accounts a rational form of personal investment, and the system of giving semiannual bonuses, amounting to as much as five months' salary, encourages all workers to save. Inadequate social security benefits in Japan are a further incentive to save for old age and for educating children. Finally, the pervasive American practice of buying on credit and obtaining loans has yet to infiltrate Japan, thereby necessitating the accumulation of needed funds before buying.

Japan's industrial investment levels have also far surpassed those of the other industrialized countries. In 1978 its total gross fixed capital formation as a percentage of GNP was 30.2 percent, compared to 21.5 percent for West Germany, 21.5 percent for France, 18.1 percent for the United Kingdom, and 18.1 percent for the United States. More importantly, Japanese investments are made primarily in high-priority and growth industries.

These high rates of investment in capital equipment and plant are facilitated by the Japanese financing system, primarily by means of massive bank credits. Since capital needs of the expanding economy far exceed the resources of Japanese commercial banks, these banks draw regularly and permanently on the funds of the Bank of Japan for lending operations. Because the Ministry of Finance controls the Bank of Japan, national enterprises enjoy access to the entire lending power of the government, at least for those business activities that contribute to articulated economic objectives. Furthermore the Bank of Japan traditionally has set low interest rates on its loans, a practice that permits and even encourages Japanese firms to assume debt-to-equity ratios of four-to-one or more. Consequently Japanese industry frequently is leveraged by as much as 80 percent, compared to about 40 percent in the United States. It is not unusual for Japanese banks to own voting stock in client firms (typically up to 5 percent), and this permits them to monitor industrial management. In the United States, persons with equity interest in a corporation have limited leverage on industrial management. Also interest rates are not as low as some American observers have argued. Japanese banks typically extend short-term loans to firms, which in effect become long-term loans when renewed or rolled over, but the interest charged is then as much or more than U.S. firms have had to pay (until the recent skyrocketing of interest rates in the United States in 1979-1980).

The leveraging of debt by Japanese corporations, reinforced by liberal lending policies and Japanese government support of R&D for commercial applications, has been important to the risk affinities of certain Japanese firms that might otherwise be more conservative in their commitments to technological change. (Yet Sony and Matsushita, both high-risk takers and late arrivers in the Japanese economy, have uncharacteristically low debt-to-equity ratios.) The willingness of Japanese stockholders to realize long-term returns from growth stocks rather than high ongoing dividends takes the pressure off Japanese industrial management to show quick profits, the very opposite of tendencies among U.S. industrial managers. The availability of investment capital to Japanese management is enhanced by the fact that interest is a pretax expense, whereas dividends are an after-tax drain. (In the early 1970s, Japanese firms were distributing to their shareholders an average 38 percent of after-tax earnings, as compared to 52 percent for U.S. corporations, according to the Boston Consulting Group.)

Another important underpinning of the Japanese economy has been its literate, well-educated labor force. At the time of the Meiji Restoration (1868), Japan boasted a higher literacy rate than the United States or Western Europe has today. Japan enjoys the highest literacy rate in the world (99.8 percent), and the percentage of the population completing secondary education is far greater than that of its closest rivals, the United States and Canada. Graduates from Japan's nine hundred universities and colleges have doubled in number over the past decade, with perhaps the sharpest rise being in engineering and economics. Thus Japanese manufacturers can draw from a large pool of extremely well-educated youth in recruiting new workers. These new workers are brought into Japanese enterprises at relatively low wages under the seniority system and are advanced in salary at a relatively moderate rate, thus ensuring an ample supply of technical and managerial skills at low cost to the corporation.

In addition to being highly literate, Japanese workers are also strongly motivated, a trait derived from the national tradition of group loyalty. In Japan, social and ethical instruction subordinates individual achievement to the attainment of group objectives. The effort an individual makes reflects on his family, school, company, and ultimately on Japan. The will to succeed for Japan is reinforced by the paternalistic nature of the corporation and the practice of lifetime employment.

Perhaps the most significant ingredient of Japanese industrial competitiveness has been its ability to design and engineer industrial products and production systems and effectively manage them at successive stages of market growth. As wages have risen, Japan has maintained its competitiveness in world markets through continuing rationalization and modernization of its industrial plants and production methods, progressively improving its cost-effectiveness through constant value engineering of components and parts and improvement of overall product design. In large part these achievements have been possible due to the other factors of Japan's growth—the quality and productivity of its labor force and management, the high rate of investment in installed plant and equipment, and a financial environment conducive to risk taking in long-term technology innovation.

U.S. and European firms made substantial contributions to Japanese technological advance through the patent licensing process in the 1950s and 1960s. These agreements laid a sound base from which Japanese enterprise moved into world markets in the 1970s. U.S. firms, such as RCA, viewed licensing as an additional revenue source in selling their technology to Japanese firms. But they underestimated the Japanese ability to absorb basic technology and, with significant supplemental improvements, to compete with U.S. firms. With the industrial foundation laid, for example, in the steel, electronic component (including semiconductors), and certain precision-parts industries (including machine tool, camera, and related optical industries), Japanese enterprise has attained the capability to produce quality products at costs that U.S. industry has found increasingly difficult to match. In an increasing number of industrial sectors, by the time U.S. firms realize they are being overtaken by Japanese industry, it is too late to regain the lost ground. U.S. firms now purchase Japanese-made parts, disassemble them, and find they cannot match Japanese production costs for critical componentry.

A related source of Japanese competitiveness in the world economy has been its explicit recognition of comparative advantage as a dynamic process and one closely linked with progressive technological development. Thus we have witnessed successive waves of sector development in Japan, moving to the technology-intensive and higher domestic value-added industries and away from the low-skill and materials-consuming industries. For example, although Japan was producing both textiles and automobiles in the late 1960s more cheaply than any other nation, it realized that in the future it could enhance its comparative advantage in automobile production through superior scale and technology and that it would eventually lose its competitiveness in textiles. This insight guided Japan's gradual rationalization and withdrawal from textiles and its increased commitment to automobile production.

The economy's ability to respond rapidly to technical and economic change is in part a function of the industry-government relationship. Industry and government in the United States and other industrialized countries have yet to come to such harmonious arrangements.

A final and important underpinning of the Japanese economy is its dual structure. Underlying and often buttressing the huge corporations, such as Mitsubishi, Toyota, and Hitachi, is a dense stratum of small to tiny firms, performing a variety of functions for the large corporation sector, the most important of which includes parts supply, mechanical work and finishing operations, and the provision of contract labor to large manufacturers. In an almost total reversal of the U.S. industrial employment pattern, Japan's manufacturing labor force is heavily concentrated in small industry (defined in Japanese terms as firms with under three hundred employees). Approximately 70 percent of all Japanese production workers, compared with 40 percent in the United States, are employed in this sector.

An attractive feature of the small-scale structure is competitive production costs, given the wide wage and benefit differentials between large and small firms in Japan. (Although wage costs are lower in the small-industry sector, productivity rates are also lower.) In addition, the availability of added capacity that these smaller firms offer gives a major company valuable flexibility both in the variety of products it assembles and the speed with which it can shift production loads among them.[1] Firms in the small-scale sector rarely operate independently; rather they act in symbiosis with the larger companies. Many are informally or formally incorporated under larger companies, which serve not only as the primary market for their output but also as a source of technical assistance and credit. Matsushita Electric Industrial Co., Ltd., for example, has more than five hundred such affiliates supporting its operations. There are also tiers of firms, with a descending order of attachment and dependence. The comparative advantage enjoyed by many of the small- and medium-sized labor-intensive Japanese firms has been partially eroded in recent years by increased production costs and operating overhead, but they still make a perceptible contribution to Japanese competitiveness in world markets and account for much of the economy's resiliency to technical and economic change.

Over 40 percent of the overseas operations undertaken between 1950 and 1970 were by what the Japanese term small-size firms. Larger Japanese firms often preempt the domestic market, forcing smaller firms to concentrate on export markets (with the help of thousands of trading companies and the technical and credit support of the Japanese government).

Government-Industry Relations

Government-industry relations in Japan have contributed immeasurably to the international competitiveness of Japanese industry. The Japanese government has combined carrots of fiscal incentives and protection during infant industry stages with sticks of continuing pressures on Japanese industry to rationalize production through mergers, technical upgrading of production methods, retraining of industrial workers, and a variety of other programs. A high degree of cooperation and consultation among government, industry, and the banking community helps to define common objectives in particular sectors and in the formulation of consensual action.

These arrangements contrast dramatically with the multiplicity of purpose and initiative that characterizes the U.S. economy and society and that may have contributed to our strengths in the past but is proving to be a disadvantage in a rapidly changing world economy that includes formidable commercial adversaries. The U.S. government has responded to pressure groups who are demanding protection as foreign competition intensifies without having the countervailing leverage or means to induce segments of U.S. industry to improve their competitive efficiencies or be phased out, which has been the situation in Japan for several decades. Nor do we have the coordinated mechanisms among government, business, and financial communities to manage or significantly influence adjustments to economic and technical change in the world economy, now occurring at a much more rapid and far-reaching level than in the past.

In contrast to the U.S. situation, where firms effectively are prevented by antitrust provisions from consultative or collaborative effort to reorganize or restructure an industrial sector faced with the onslaught of foreign competition, Japanese firms are allowed considerable leeway and even given government support in coordinating and implementing sector plans for technological upgrading (including combined research efforts), mergers, or other concerted efforts aimed at rationalizing an industry and adjusting competitively to market changes. The Japanese are very effective at harmonized action, while our traditional reliance on marketplace adjustments, often distorted by government interference, is proving inadequate by comparison. This cultural ability to rationalize production in the economy as a whole is an important fundamental source of Japanese competitiveness.

Government funding of R&D is another area of distinct advantage for Japan. Beginning in the early 1950s, particular sectors of Japanese industry have benefited from favored treatment by the Japanese government at successive stages of economic development, ranging from special lines of capital expansion credit to joint funding of R&D costs and infant industry protection. Steel, shipbuilding, automobile, and most recently computer equipment are outstanding cases in point. Japanese government support of R&D efforts estimated at $230 million in the computer equipment field, has concentrated on developing commercial prototypes that can be manufactured competitively. This effort stands in marked contrast to U.S. government funding, where more than half of the industrial research over the past decade has gone into development of defense and space prototypes, which generally require considerable additional funding for commercial adaptations and even more to design and engineer for U.S. production. Thus U.S. enterprises are at a substantial competitive disadvantage in relation to the Japanese in regard to governmental funding of commercial prototypes for international markets.

Existing U.S. capital-gains tax regulations also place Japanese firms at a competitive advantage relative to their U.S. counterparts. U.S. firms, particularly those now facing intense import competition, find themselves compelled to move out of initially low-profit, high-risk, and technology-intensive products. These product areas often require considerable investments in R&D and new plant and equipment to maintain competitiveness, and their prospects for earnings materialize only in the long run. U.S. firms increasingly are drawn toward alternative products that require only a limited technological effort and where the corporation's marketing position and skills are a dominant factor. Existing U.S. capital-gains tax regulations in effect encourage these shifts to low-risk product and service profit centers by not giving sufficient weight or preferential treatment to the high-risk costs of R&D and retooling of plant and equipment. In contrast the Japanese tax system gives high rewards to business innovators and risk takers, with virtually tax-free accumulation of capital gains.[2]

Interventions and Policies

The government-industry relationship in Japan plays a major role in the formulation process and effectiveness of Japan's economic policy, yet there are widespread misconceptions and misapprehensions about the process on the part of many Westerners. Briefly the relationship can be characterized as a participatory partnership among different segments of government and industry, based upon pragmatic considerations and mutual respect, working for goals generally agreed upon.

The relationship typically has been referred to as Japan, Inc., a not-altogether inappropriate label in that its inner workings are somewhat analogous to the operations of today's giant, multidivisional, highly diversified corporation. (The label is inappropriate, however, in the context of a hierarchical and monolithic corporate headquarters.) The various components of Japan, Inc., be they industrial sectors or individual firms, operate as autonomous units and seek to maximize their efficiency and profitability and to enhance their competitiveness both at home and abroad. At the same time, the government, in its role as top management and having access to the resources of the entire combination, can coordinate, through consensus creation, the various component operations to yield maximum return for the Japanese nation.[3]

In this regard, the Japanese government is not content to defer to market forces alone to achieve a sustained high level of performance of the economy but is committed to a policy of intervention. There has been an unrelenting effort to move people and resources into prospective comparative advantage areas with promising high growth rate and productivity potential and to encourage the phase-out of declining or poor-performance industries. This concern over the maintenance of competition and over the survival of the fittest industries and firms sets Japanese government policy apart from the indicative planning as practiced in France, for example.

Although the phenomenon today called Japan, Inc., is decidedly a post-World War II development, there are historical antecedents to this unique relationship between government and industry dating back to 1868, the time of the Meiji Restoration. After two and a half centuries of isolation from the rest of the world, the Meiji government deliberately and authoritatively undertook to industrialize a very backward Japan. The undertaking was greatly facilitated by the already well-established cultural tradition of vertical symbiosis in Japan, of patronage down and loyalty up. In contrast to European countries at the time, there was no need in Japan for the government to intervene on the grounds of class equality; it justified its action on the purely pragmatic ground that Japan was far behind the other economies of the world and that the government had in place, through its bureaucracy, an able and efficient organization that could oversee and intervene in the industrialization process.

Government interaction in the economy in this earlier period was more direct and central than it has ever been in the twentieth century (with the exception of World War II). The government assumed control and responsibility for financing industry, organizing factors of production, and directing trade. Gradually the functions of finance and production were turned back to the private sector. This reinforcing and satisfying experience in Japan's history helps explain its preparedness to permit the government to play such a pivotal role in the economy today.

Structural Organization

The central economic policy-making role of the Japanese government resides in the Economic Planning Agency of the prime minister's office, which does long-range planning for economic growth and identifies where government support and action can best advance these plans. Based in part on these long-range plans and coupled with close consultation with academicians, consumer groups, and industry (the last through advisory committees composed of business leaders and through business groups), the ministries and various independent agencies formulate their own plans. The ministries also issue white papers on a variety of public-policy issues impinging on industrial activity, and these are perceived as guides by government agencies, trade associations, and individual firms. Directives (or as they are more commonly called, administrative guidelines) issued by the government agencies themselves are perceived similarly. Although there is no legal or compulsory status attached to these government communications, they are more or less observed, with a few rare exceptions, in both spirit and letter by the financial, commercial, and industrial communities in Japan, provided there is at least a minimal amount of consensus between government and industry views.

At the heart of the policy guidelines is a commitment to concentrate available resources in areas of fastest growth in demand and highest productivity. Responsibility for implementing the guidelines resides principally in two institutions: the Ministry of Finance and the Ministry of International Trade and Industry (MITI). The Ministry of Finance is the prime and ultimate source of financing for industrial investment in Japan and has close links with the banking system. If the financial community is to maintain and expand Japan's industrial growth, it must make accurate judgments as to where the growth opportunities lie in the economy. And for these accurate judgments, the Ministry of Finance relies heavily upon guidelines from MITI, each of whose bureaus closely monitors a particular sector in the economy. The guidelines developed by MITI strongly influence the lending operations of government-owned banks. MITI's judgments, in turn, are reinforced by a plethora of policy tools it has at its disposal to encourage (but rarely force) certain Japanese industries to move in the direction it believes most desirable for the economy as a whole. MITI, of course, does not have complete autonomy in this area and does find itself in conflict with other ministries, particularly Finance, from time to time, but it does act as the principal architect of Japanese industrial policy.

Policy Instruments

The Japanese government, through MITI or any other agency, does not issue directive and commands for immediate action and compliance by industry; rather it communicates its goals to industry through an intricate set of incentives and indirect controls. In frequency of use, carrots definitely outweigh sticks, but neither is used to assert government primacy. Instead they are designed to make adherence to common goals fruitful and practical. Import licenses, control over use of foreign exchange, capital depreciation allowances, tax and reserve policies, government loans and subsidies, relaxation of antitrust regulations, and export allowances all act as both controls in the negative sense and as incentives. In the early phase of industrial development (until the mid-1950s), the Japanese government pursued deliberate policies of orchestrated protection of infant industries, screening foreign investment and licensing to prevent the entry of preemptive foreign enterprise. As a further contribution to advancing productivity, economic authorities have sought to channel savings and investments into capital, technology, and human resource development.

The most efficient allocation of resources is of paramount importance to the Japanese government. Economic authorities have applied carrots and sticks to phase out textiles, toys, and certain optical instruments and to channel resources into high-performance industries such as optical fibers, computers, automobile production, and office machinery. Capital resources are extended to industries such as chemicals and certain home electric appliances where productivity is high but absolute growth rates relatively low. The computer and aircraft industries had annual growth rates of 20 to 25 percent in the late 1960s, but productivity gains were relatively low; these industries thus attracted government R&D funds to raise output.

Illustrations of the Relationship

The system works best in cases where consensus on basic goals and tactics can be reached. Let us consider briefly two different industries in Japan, automobile production and steel, which have responded in very different ways to Japanese government attempts to influence their development. The government's interest in the former dates back to the 1950s when it sought to rationalize the motor vehicle industry by consolidating both the parts sector and the automobile producers. MITI's desire to rationalize the industry, however, far exceeded the willingness and ability of the companies concerned. For example, MITI's objective was to reduce the number of primary parts manufacturers to forty-five in order to achieve certain economies of scale. Today there are still over three hundred such companies operating in Japan. MITI's real problems and more-notable failures, however, occurred in its efforts to restructure the automobile producers themselves.

The first resistance by the auto manufacturers to government policy arose in 1955 when MITI proposed that the companies cooperatively develop a prototype "People's Car" and then permit MITI to select one design and subsidize its production by a single manufacturer. The automakers quietly but effectively opposed such a plan, particularly the selection and subsidization of a single company, and the plan failed to reach the Diet (the Japanese legislative branch).

MITI pursued its objective of consolidating the industry in 1961 with a proposal to the Industrial Structure Advisory Board that passenger car production be organized into groups, based on the car's basic type of design. With the exception of Toyota and Nissan, the industry again was opposed to the plan. One merger had been achieved—that of the auto firm Prince into Nissan Auto—but due primarily to close family relations. In addition to avoiding bankruptcy for Prince, which was then in a weakened financial position, Nissan also badly needed the additional passenger car capacity that Prince's modern and underutilized plant could provide. But MITI made little progress in urging the other auto companies to consolidate. The companies were all profitable, and it is usually under conditions where one company is suffering declining earnings or where another, larger company stands to diversify its product line or increase capacity that merger orders are most attractive.

There was strong interest in the late 1960s to link Isuzu Motors with another Japanese motor-vehicle producer. Four separate auto-producer agreements were negotiated (Fuji-Isuzu in 1966, Mitsubishi-Fuji-Isuzu in 1967, Mitsubishi-Isuzu in 1967, and Nissan-Isuzu in 1968), but not one was consummated. Instead Mitsubishi entered into a joint venture with Chrysler as its minority partner, and Isuzu negotiated a similar arrangement with General Motors. (A recent General Motors advertisement in *Business Week* asked American consumers, "Why buy a Japanese car when you can buy a General Motors' car manufactured in Japan?" (by Isuzu).

The Japanese automobile industry is an example not only of conflicting objectives between government and industry but also of a divergence in goals among ministries of the government. Various ministries were undecided after World War II as to whether Japan should develop a domestic auto industry. (As late as 1958-1959, the government was offering Ford and General Motors the opportunity to come into Japan on a 49 percent minority-share basis.) The Bank of Japan in particular opposed developing the industry, arguing that the economy lacked a comparative advantage in auto production and that it would never become competitive in world markets. The policy debate continued for two years before it was resolved in a determination to fund and encourage the nascent trucking industry to diversify into car manufacture.

The experience of the steel industry has been radically different; in fact, the best evidence for the belief that Japanese business and government leaders share common goals and an understanding of how best to achieve them can be found in the country's steel-making sector. The industry has been at the heart of Japan's postwar economic success and has accounted in large part for the competitiveness of Japan's major industrial exports—ships, autos, bearings, and machinery—in world markets.

Cooperative relations date back before World War II and during the war when the government actually controlled the steel industry in Japan. This cooperation continued after the war because both parties keenly recognized the need to restore the industry's production and to secure raw materials. The government provided financial assistance to the industry through enhanced access to lending sources, and it devised fiscal incentives designed to encourage growth by individual producers. With the exception of the immediate postwar recovery subsidies (which were of sizable proportions), however, the Japanese government has not played a principal or direct role in modern Japan's steel industry development.

The government's major concern has been to circumscribe and influence the capacity expansion decisions of private producers who, since the mid-1950s, have shown a tendency to increase production capacity too quickly. MITI's efforts to restrain and reconcile the varying growth ambitions of the steel manufacturers have been its greatest contribution to the industry. For limited periods of time and for specific product items, it has reorganized the companies into cartel producers in order to avoid price instability by moderating production levels. The ministry has played but a marginal role in most other areas, such as the securing of long-term raw-material supply sources and the voluntary control of exports. Its role in the control of exports has increased in recent years, however, due to the protests by European and American steel makers against Japanese imports. The Ministry of Finance has also been active in the Japanese steel industry through financing its growth. The Fair Trade Commission, whose responsibility it is to interpret the Japanese antimonopoly law, has been active as well; it opposed the MITI-backed merger between the Fuji and Yawata steel companies in 1969-1970.

Some have attributed the extent of consensus between government and steel industry leaders to the presence of retired bureaucrats in top-management positions of the steel companies. Someone who has spent a career in the civil service may lack certain business experience but is recognized as a valuable channel of communication to government authorities. Another source of consensus today between Japan's steel industry and government is the continuity of senior management, many of whom began their careers in the industry when it was under government control (this is particularly true for Nippon Steel).

The automobile and steel industries illustrate the extremes of where Japan, Inc., operates and where it does not. Clearly the Japanese are able to establish consensus and symbiotic relationships within and between industries in order to achieve growth, with or without formal government-industry cooperation. Government-industry consensus serves as an additional spur to growth. It has been said that consensus is reached in Japan not through rational decision making but rather through an intuitive process, a concept alien to most Westerners. We do know that when there is a consensus, it works well and strongly reinforces Japanese competitiveness in world markets. The Japan, Inc., system stands in stark contrast to the adversary relationship that typically prevails between U.S. industry and government.

Enterprise Organization and Management

The enterprise system in Japan incorporates several features that contribute to the health of the economy and its competitiveness in world markets: Japanese management philosophy and objectives, the financial structure of its industry, and the generally harmonious and mutually supportive relationship that prevails between management and labor. Combined, these features permit Japanese enterprises to assume a high-risk and aggressive stance in their R&D and marketing efforts, to change product designs and manufacturing techniques rapidly and efficiently to meet competition, and to maintain high rates of productivity.

Industrial Structure

The dual sector economy still survives in Japan. A high-volume, capital-intensive sector pays its labor force a higher level of wages and characteristically provides lifetime employment; the other sector is a widespread network of small factories and job shops, which pay lower wages to a fluctuating labor force. These small factories are able to furnish high-quality precision components and parts at competitive cost and with relatively modest investments in plant and equipment. This labor-intensive sector is able to substitute a relatively high level of artisan skills for the precision and quality control that typically is built into high-volume, automated equipment. (It is this segment of small- to medium-size firms that is able to move offshore to low-wage developing countries and adapt most effectively their low-technology, labor-intensive range of production techniques to local skills and capabilities.) These supplier industries provide an added flexibility and versatility to Japan's industrial economy.

Interviews with Japanese firms that now operate plant facilities in the United States reveal certain distinct differences between U.S. and Japanese factory-manning structures that give Japanese industries a distinct advantage. One difference is that there is a much narrower range of industry in the United States than there is in Japan where factory skills can be substituted for machines and computerized control systems. Another difference is that both sectors of Japan's dual-sector economy employ a higher ratio of engineers and other technical personnel to factory workers relative to the U.S. manufacturing enterprises. (Sony, one of several Japanese firms that operate plants in the United States, indicated this difference may be as high as five-to-one at the operational level, where there is an intensive interaction between technicians and production supervisors and operators. About two-thirds of these Japanese technicians are university trained.) These differences in factory-manning structures place a heavy burden on U.S. firms to invest in product and process design and engineering and upon related investments in automation and other technical upgrading of plant or equipment if the U.S. industrial base is to maintain its rate of productivity gain at a sufficient level to continue to compete effectively with Japanese firms' production.

Lifetime employment in the more-advanced (capital-intensive) sector of Japan's economy, coupled with a social structure that is more amenable to fluctuation in industrial employment levels in the labor-intensive sector (reinforced by the relatively high rate of growth for the economy as a whole, which has been able to absorb excess labor, by and large), have helped to facilitate the introduction of automation in response to world competition and the shifting of production to new product areas as market opportunities are recognized.

The lifetime employment system extends up to a mandatory retirement age of fifty-seven to sixty. More importantly, however, there is a psychological contract between managers and employees to the effect that the former do not let their mistakes regarding misreading of market trends or designing of bad products result in workers' layoff. Although only large firms can afford to extend management's commitment to rank-and-file workers, both male and female, even small firms adhere to this psychological contract. This is why workers do not oppose automation or the introduction of new products. In times of economic crisis, this management-employee relation has proven to be very effective. Managers and workers close ranks and cut salaries and fringe benefits to avoid more severe measures.

Rotational assignments among departments and plants within the larger industrial complexes of Japan give managers and technicians the necessary experience and versatility to facilitate shifts. The imperative to automate in Japan is reinforced by a growing shortage of low-wage factory labor and an expanding percentage of university-trained engineers and other technical people, who provide Japanese industry with the design-engineering capability that is now used intensively to expand Japan's competitiveness in world trade.

Design-Engineering Capabilities

The ability to design and engineer products that meet market demands and can be manufactured competitively under the emerging Japanese industrial environment has been a trademark of Japanese enterprises and perhaps their primary source of competitiveness in the world economy. This evolving capability has enabled Japan to move progressively into increasingly complex and sophisticated production and to utilize effectively their widespread network of small-scale parts suppliers to penetrate internationally competitive markets.

Broad segments of Japanese industry are aggressive in the development of new and diversified product lines that are tailored to the specialized demands of different world markets. Product lines have been progressively redesigned for high-volume quality production as Japanese enterprises have moved down the learning curve. Japanese firms benefited from the widespread, synergistic effects of being able to design and engineer for Japanese production, beginning with generally less-efficient, low-volume methods and later moving on to successive generations of higher-volume, interrelated components and end products, always updating and improving upon earlier production experiences. In the color television field, there was an early emphasis upon low-energy-input, high-performance, zero-defect products, which are realized by such means.

Strategic Objectives and Global Marketing Strategies

Japanese management philosophy is best described as a powerful commitment to growth and a long-range strategy in pursuing the company's interest.

The commitment to growth derives from a real understanding and practice of the learning-curve principle, a principle certainly understood by American firms but only rarely incorporated into production or marketing strategies (with but a few exceptions, most notably, Texas Instruments). Briefly this principle states that real unit costs tend to decline with the accumulation of production experience. (Some pioneering work has been done on the learning curve principle by the Boston Consulting Group. Their extensive study of cost-volume relationships indicates that real unit costs in any industry decline at a fairly constant rate each time the production experience doubles. The rate of decline varies from one industry to another depending on several factors, such as capital intensivity of the production.)

The leading Japanese firms have based their growth strategies, in large part, upon exploiting the close relationship between the internal and the external market. Products introduced to the home market are carefully selected and designed with a view toward achieving rapid growth and large production volumes early in the product cycle. In contrast, marketing efforts by American firms are often a matter of using advertising, discounting, or publicity to create a demand for a product already developed. The consequent economies of scale achieved enable Japanese companies to reduce costs sufficiently to enter export markets. In turn, expansion of market penetration overseas helps to increase domestic scale still further and thereby enhance productivity.

Japanese commitments to global market expansion are evident in the characteristic growth rates enjoyed by Japanese enterprises. Through the 1970s, the typical manufacturing concern increased its sales at compound rates of between 15 and 25 percent annually, translating to a doubling of sales every three to five years. Japanese enterprises in this situation are almost always installing additional capacity. In a high-growth context, market share rather than absolute numerical performance becomes a crucial measure. Failure to meet demand through a lack of capacity or uncompetitive pricing results quickly in a loss of market. These pressures are exacerbated by the accelerated life cycle that products demonstrate in Japan. Both consumer and industrial products tend to move more rapidly from introduction to market saturation in Japan than they do in the United States. For example, the color television market in Japan had reached a much higher saturation point by 1972 than had the U.S. market, even though color television was introduced in Japan several years after it was in the United States.

The aggressive push into export markets serves Japanese enterprise not only in increasing volume but also in providing an outlet for temporary overcapacity. Faced with fixed costs, such as labor and interest charges, which do not vary with levels of output, the typical large Japanese manufacturer has a strong incentive to export temporary excess production until domestic demand catches up. It is this phenomenon that underlies the observation that Japanese exports are stepped up at times of recession, as they are currently, and are constricted during economic recovery or abnormally high-growth periods. Highly competitive pricing of exports also accompanies the periods of slow domestic growth.

When Japanese firms move into world markets, which they often do very rapidly, they adjust product design configurations to meet overseas demands. U.S. efforts to capture and service external markets are feeble by comparison. In contrast to American companies, Japanese firms are highly attuned to their worldwide customers' demands. The parochial market vision of U.S. firms accounts for their failure to penetrate the Japanese color television market in the early 1960s when they still had the necessary technological lead. Japanese penetration of U.S. color television markets is due to the aggressive drive of Japanese enterprises and their willingness to adapt product designs and serve customer demands beyond what U.S. firms have been willing to do.

Another distinguishing characteristic of Japanese management is its attention to the long-range competitive position of the firm and the relative lack of concern over short-run profitability indicators. This difference in attitude, for example, is demonstrated in the practice of measuring corporate growth in terms of market share rather than total sales. Proposed new investments are evaluated with a view toward their provision of a sound basis for the long-term growth of the firm.

Taking this long-term approach, Japanese firms have become highly versatile and commercially effective in operating up and down the product cycle—evolving manufacturing expertise from the less-sophisticated products and components to the more-complex and profitable items. This is how they were able to advance in just ten years from the manufacture of small black-and-white television sets to small-size and later larger-size color television, and eventually to preempt completely the videotape recorder (VTR) manufacturing field. U.S. firms unwittingly have accommodated Japanese business strategies by yielding the mature end of product lines more rapidly than they should have and moving offshore rather than redesigning and reengineering production techniques and new product generations to meet Japanese competition. Japanese firms have also moved to offshore sites (in Taiwan and Singapore), but they have done this both to facilitate a shift in Japan to higher-technology component production and to provide alternative bases for penetrating the U.S. market.

Japanese industry also has been highly successful in penetrating U.S. marketing and distribution channels. They have successfully outflanked U.S. firms with their own marketing and distribution channels or in collaboration with high-volume retailers such as Sears. The preference some U.S. manufacturers have shown for exclusive franchises (with relatively high markup) has proven to be another competitive disadvantage.

Labor-Management Relations

Attributable in large part to the unique employment system, relations between management and labor in Japanese enterprise are amicable and mutually supportive. Although the system is strained today due to the prolonged recession in Japan, a majority of large firms still follow the lifetime employment practice for both workers and salaried employees. Career progress is still determined primarily by education and seniority. Most workers are hired immediately after completing their education and become, in effect, a member of the corporate family, assuming the mutual obligations and rights that are implicit in such a relationship.

Permanence of employment and the seniority-based wage work reinforce the fastest-growing sectors of the economy and, at the same time, put pressure on the slower-growing and less-efficient industries. Since pay is a function of age, a rapidly growing enterprise that draws from an employment pool of youthful graduates benefits from low labor costs and recently trained workers who are familiar with the latest techniques. In addition, due to difficulties in recruiting from outside the company, rapidly growing firms tend to delegate responsibility to younger and, presumably, more aggressive people.

Workers typically are organized into company unions. Consequently strikes are infrequent and usually only of symbolic value, so that the company is rarely in the position of having to default on orders due to labor-management disputes. One other major advantage of the lifetime employment system is the relative ease with which new technologies, particularly those that are labor saving, can be introduced to the manufacturing process. Employees have no fear that the new processes will result in job loss or pay reductions because they are retrained for other technical, management, or sales positions. Instead the logic of technological innovation is compelling to Japanese at all levels of the corporation: improved products manufactured more efficiently mean that the company will grow, and the company's growth, in turn, will make possible a higher standard of living for each individual contributing to the process. Dependence on continued and rapid growth for maintaining high employment levels, however, has begun to cause concern for the future of Japanese labor among many government and industry leaders.

This description of the Japanese employment system applies essentially to large firms in the modern industries and almost exclusively to male workers. Women in general and workers in small- to medium-sized industry in Japan do not enjoy such benefits or job security. The labor force in this sector, however, is another important source of flexibility for the large corporation, which can tap this reservoir of labor when demand exceeds the company's immediate capacity, without incurring the attendant obligations to the workers.

Japanese employment practices, and in fact, its entire enterprise system not only work best under conditions of high growth but actually serve to promote rapid growth of the economy. A high-growth environment facilitates long-term perspective on company operations and the heavy use of debt financing. In turn, sustained growth points to market share rather than absolute sales as the significant indicator of performance. This encourages further financing of business with debt and the additional hiring of new graduates. All of these actions reinforce the competitiveness of the enterprise: aggressive investment and pricing policies are dictated by the high value attached to market share, debt financing permits the separation of growth from profits, and a lower average age work force reduces the labor costs. The elements of the system are dynamic and interdependent, with growth acting as the prime catalyst.

Japan today, however, is not in a high-growth period, and there are tremendous pressures on the employment system. Some economic analysts in Japan argue that the system, in fact, is the nation's single largest brake on business expansion. Officially about 1.3 million workers, representing 2.1 percent of the labor force, were without jobs in 1980, but some analysts assert that the real unemployment rate may have been as high as 6 percent because private firms are carrying up to 3 million unnecessary workers on their payrolls. Although this practice saves the government much revenue in unemployment compensation, it burdens Japanese companies with an additional financial load of an estimated $20 billion a year, money that could be used for capital investment.[4]

Financing Industrial Growth

Capital for new investment or expansion is relatively accessible to Japanese firms through bank loans. It is not unusual for a Japanese manufacturer to have a debt-to-equity ratio of three- or four- to one. Debt ratios on this order mean that Japanese companies need not finance their growth out of retained earnings. Once they have earned enough to cover the interest on their debt, there is little financial constraint on their growth. And the interest charges, particularly to large industrial firms, are relatively low.

Capitalization through debt financing is quite acceptable, and even preferable in Japan due in large part to the fact that the stock market in Japan is an expensive and unreliable source of financing. Traditionally stock is issued at par rather than at market value, and the sale of stock thus yields less cash. In addition, due to the cyclical nature of the Japanese stock market since World War II, investments by shareholders have traditionally been risky and hence required a high rate of return on equity (10 to 15 percent). Individual shareholders in Japan, however, put little pressure on companies to issue scheduled dividends. The significance of ease of access to low-cost capital, coupled with relative freedom from shareholder demands, is considerable in terms of a company's ability to assume high technical or marketing risks in corporate decisions and to plan for long-range growth and profitability.

It is commonly believed that Japanese enterprises are not as profitable as their Western counterparts, based on conventional comparisons of income statements. The bottom line for reading U.S. corporate earnings is net profit after taxes. This figure generally is higher in American firms, but it fails to take into account retained cash flow after dividend payments and Japanese accounting rules permitting the retention of reserves.

Japanese firms that have used equity financing have traditionally paid out much lower dividends than have their U.S. counterparts. This is in part due to an economic growth rate much higher than that of United States and a resulting need to retain more cash for expansion, as well as Japanese investors' understanding of the individual enterprise's need to keep the earnings and defer dividend payments. The Japanese accounting device of reserves is designed to shield income from taxes. Income used for purposes such as retirement funds, overseas investment losses, or accelerated depreciation can be placed in reserves on which taxes are deferred but not altogether exempted. For companies experiencing constant growth, these tax deferrals provide a permanent source of cash. When these two factors are introduced into income statements, Japanese firms tend to show slightly greater levels of retained cash as a percentage of total sales, which is of far greater importance for maintaining enterprise competitiveness than short-run profitability.

Notes

1. Yoshi Tsurumi also refers to this characteristic of Japanese industrial structure. See the case of *Singer*. v. *Japanese Sewing Machine* in *The Japanese Are Coming* (Cambridge, Mass.: Ballinger Publishing Co., 1976), pp. 24-27. This vertical structure also serves to reinforce the export-led discipline of price and quality.

2. See Joseph A. Pechman and Keimei Kaizuka, "Taxation," in *Asia's New Giant: How the Japanese Economy Works*, ed. Hugh Patrick and Henry Rosovsky (Washington, D.C.: The Brookings Institution, 1976), pp. 362-364. Pechman and Kaizuka point out, however, that the Japanese tax system uses no unusual technique to help maintain business and management incentives in Japan.

3. A recent monograph on this subject characterizes the Japanese government's role as essentially one of providing the opportunity and

framework for business development. See Caryl A. Callahan, "Business-Government Relations in Japan," in *Japan Module* (New York: Japan Society, 1980).

4. Whether lifetime employment is, on balance, viewed as a boon or a bane depends in part on one's overall view and evaluation of this aspect of the Japanese industrial system. We are indebted to Yoshi Tsurumi for the following observation: "I would like to take strong issue with your passing implication that Japanese firms are burdened with this disguised employment. You have to take a larger view. From the government's viewpoint, the choice is either to let firms carry them (and tax firms less) or to let the government carry them through higher taxation of firms (as in the U.S. case). For one, I advocate the policy to let firms carry workers and retrain them and tax them less. This system is far more conducive to technological innovations and growth."

Part II
Japan's Consumer-Electronics Industry

The Japanese Industry

Production and Markets

Japan today is the largest producer of consumer electronics and the second largest producer of all types of electronic equipment in the Western world. The country's peak year in production of color television was 1976; it manufactured 10.5 million units, up by almost 20 percent over the previous peak production level of 8.8 million units in 1973. Yet in 1979 color television production in Japan totaled 9,830,352 units. As in the United States, the number of producers in Japan has declined over the past fifteen years. In 1963 there were twenty-two manufacturers; in 1970, eighteen; in 1972, fifteen; and today there are only ten.

The major Japanese manufacturers of color television receivers are Matsushita Electric Industrial Co., Ltd.; Sony Corporation; Tokyo Shibaura Electric Co., Ltd. (Toshiba); Hitachi Ltd.; Tokyo Sanyo Electric Industry Co., Ltd.; Mitsubishi Electric Corporation; Sharp Corporation; General Corporation; Victor Company of Japan, Ltd.; and New Nippon Electric Co., Ltd. As of 1978, Matsushita was manufacturing between 23 and 25 percent of all Japanese color television sets produced; Toshiba, 13 to 16 percent; Sanyo, 12 to 13 percent; Sony, 10 to 12 percent; and Hitachi, 9 to 10 percent. By and large, manufacturers of television sets also produce the color cathode-ray tubes. In 1979 16.4 million were produced in Japan, of which 38 percent (6.2 million) were exported. The percentage of tubes exported has risen in recent years due to the increasing number of sets being manufactured overseas by Japanese firms. Yet Sharp and General purchase their color cathode-ray tubes from Toshiba, and Sanyo and Japan Victor obtain theirs from Matsushita Electric.

Ashai Glass Company and Nippon Electric Glass Company equally share the market for supplying glass tubes for color cathode-ray tubes. Denki Onkyo Co., Ltd., and Matsushita account for about one-third each of the domestic production of deflection yokes for color television receivers, with other internal suppliers providing the final third of the market. The major tuner manufacturers in Japan are Alps Electric Co., Ltd., and Mitsumi Electric, which is also doing an active business in providing electronic tuners, but it is likely that the television receiver manufacturers may begin producing their own in the future.

Domestic Demand

The Japanese domestic market for consumer electronics is the second largest in the world after the United States. Domestic demand for color television in 1978 reached approximately 5.7 million sets, a decrease over the preceding years that reflected market saturation. Although the market is still healthy, there is a considerable gap between recent domestic demand figures and the 6.5 million sets demanded in 1973, the peak year.

Market saturation for color television occurred far earlier in Japan than in the United States. By 1971 over 60 percent of Japanese urban households owned at least one color television set, compared to about 40 percent in the United States (with a population twice as large and a greater per-capita income). Approximately 95 percent of all Japanese households now own at least one color television. This means that the demand structure is now arranged in the following order: replacement of old sets, purchase of additional sets, and initial purchase of new sets.

The Japanese public has demonstrated not only a healthy appetite for consumer electronics products but also a discriminating one in terms of quality, design, and reliability. This characteristic stems from a variety of factors, including the Japanese preoccupation with conserving scarce resources and space and the high level of education, and it has forced domestic electronic manufacturers to strive to improve their products. For instance, mean time between failure for Japanese color television sets doubled between 1973 and 1976, while power consumption was halved during the same period. Low-energy input contributes to high reliability in television receivers.

The Japanese government initially protected the domestic market from foreign competition by means of a variety of tariff and nontariff barriers. A more effective and enduring protection, however, has been a lack of determination by foreign competition. Unlike the Japanese, who avidly study the cultures and languages of the United States and Western Europe, few Westerners are well informed about Japan. Thus the market potential of Japan is usually underestimated and the difficulties and risks of entering the market appear more difficult than they actually are.

Moreover Western equipment, particularly that of U.S. manufacturers, has generally been ill suited for the Japanese market. Large console-type products are not practical for crowded Japan. Since Japanese electrical codes are generally not considered at the product design stage, expensive conversion, which American firms have been generally unwilling to make, is necessary before products can be exported to Japan. Finally, Western products often lack features and accessories that are standard on Japanese equipment.

Export Performance and Strategy

A major source of growth in the Japanese television industry has been its aggressive movement into foreign markets, coupled with astute marketing tactics. In 1979 exports of color television sets, including chassis kits, reached a total of 5,559,344. Approximately 33 percent (1.8 million sets) of this total was exported to North America. Asia is the next largest export market for Japanese color televisions and accounted for 31 percent of 1979 exports (1.7 million units); South America received 16 percent of 1979 exports, Europe 11 percent, Africa 6 percent, and Oceania 3 percent. In 1979 exports of color television sets and kits to the United States (685,927 units) dropped 66 percent from the 1977 level of 2.03 million units. The sharp downturn is directly attributable to the color television Orderly Marketing Agreement (OMA), which became effective July 1, 1977. The terms of this agreement were designed to restrict the numbers of Japanese sets imported into the United States as a protection to U.S. manufacturers.

In the last year before the OMA took effect, 1976, Matsushita, Toshiba, Sanyo, and Sharp exported between 400,000 and 500,000 sets (color and black-and-white) each to the United States, Sony from 200,000 to 300,000 sets, and Hitachi and Mitsubishi 100,000 sets each. Upon the signing of the OMA, MITI assumed responsibility for allocating the designated annual quota among the Japanese exporters, using 1974 through June 1976 as a base period. The five largest—Matsushita, Sanyo, Sharp, Sony, and Toshiba—were assigned over 200,000 complete color sets each, and the remaining companies—General, Hitachi, JVC, Mitsubishi, and Nippon Electric—were allocated fewer than 100,000 apiece to export to the United States.

The constraints to further export growth in the U.S. market imposed on the Japanese companies by the OMA have compelled them to cultivate exports to other regions and to shift production to the United States. As a result, Matsushita, Sony, Sanyo, Mitsubishi, and Toshiba were all producing television sets in the United States by 1979, and Sharp and Hitachi started U.S.-based production by 1980. The principal reservations the companies had about investing in U.S. manufacture were the problems they anticipated relating to parts procurement (the import of certain major components was also severely limited by the OMA) and uncertainty about the future of American demand for color television sets.

To ensure success in the U.S. and other foreign markets, most Japanese consumer electronic products are designed to meet these markets' requirements, as well as those of the domestic market. Extensive market research is carried out in the United States and Western Europe, as well as in Japan, to find what combination of features would provide the highest combined sales. Often some additional components (and thus cost) are built in so that the product can be used in many different countries without modification. For example, Japanese products typically are designed to run on 110 volt, 60 Hz, or 220 volts, 50 Hz, simply by setting two switches. Where this approach requires too great a cost increase, the product design is manufactured in a way that allows the critical domestic and export components to be interchanged, with a minimum disruption to the production process.

The Japanese take this approach to product design because export sales are an integral part of their marketing and production strategy. The projected export volume and domestic demand are combined in planning production facilities, the higher volume justifying greater investment in automation and tooling than if only the domestic market had been considered. The greater demand also allows a pricing policy that takes into account not only the more efficient production facilities but also faster movement along the learning curve.

For Japanese enterprises, exports serve to stretch out the normal life cycle of many consumer electronics products. Initially exports represent only a small percentage of total production because domestic demand is very strong. But as saturation begins to occur and domestic demand levels off, greater emphasis is placed on exports, allowing further growth in production rates. Moreover, even when certain products become obsolescent in Japan, the manufacturer can continue to export to less-sophisticated markets. This extension of the product life cycle is another justification used for heavy investment in product design and production equipment expense.

In most product areas, exports usually go first to less-developed countries and small industrialized countries where competition is limited. The large Japanese trading companies are utilized for this sales effort, thus allowing manufacturers to limit the drain on their production and marketing resources. Meanwhile captive sales organizations in the major export markets, particularly the United States, are preparing marketing plans and materials and providing technical material to their service organizations to ensure that the product launch will go smoothly when production capacity is available and it is deemed the right time to attempt to penetrate these markets.

Although this sequence has held true for most major products such as radios, stereos, and television, significant exceptions have been CB (citizen-band) radios and videotape recorders (VTRs). Popularization of CBs in the United States occurred at a time when there was extensive underutilization of Japanese electronics manufacturing capacity and manpower. Japanese manufacturers therefore found it profitable to move into production, despite the fact that the market potential in Japan and outside the United States was very limited. VTRs represent yet another inversion of the normal

Japanese marketing strategy. Because of the high cost of VTRs, it was assumed that sales volume could be built up most quickly in the U.S. marketplace and that a strong domestic demand would develop later.

Technological Development in the Industry

Color Television

Research on color television was begun in 1928 in the West, but actual utilization did not take place until the 1950s. As early as 1932, some of the major electronic companies were experimenting with sending color images using a mechanical disc process. By the early 1940s, however, RCA, one of the leading firms, reoriented its research toward an all-electronic system. Although such a system was far from commercialization at that time, it was believed that an all-electronic system would be capable of producing a better picture on a larger screen than that produced by the mechanical swirling disc system. Second, and crucially, the all-electronic system would be compatible with any black-and-white set then existing. And since the black-and-white, all-electronic system had just been perfected, RCA felt confident of its approach. In the interim, CBS Laboratories, RCA's major competitor, had perfected the older mechanical disc process, and in a demonstration before the Federal Communications Commission (FCC) of the two systems, the mechanical system proved to have a superior picture. Hence the FCC ruled in favor of the mechanical system, incompatible to some types of black-and-white sets.

Subsequent developments indicated that the mechanical system was not economically feasible to produce. It took the FCC over three years to find its way out of the embarrassing situation of having ruled in favor of a system that nobody wanted. Finally, as a result of the recommendation of the National Television Systems Committee (NTSC), in 1953 RCA's tri-color system became the standard of the industry and became known as the NTSC system. In 1954 both NBC and CBS started actual color television broadcasting. The acceptance of color television was rather slow compared with that of black-and-white television. Not until the 1960s was it widely accepted. In 1964 the production of color television sets in the United States exceeded 1 million units and growth has been steady since then. (A more extended and detailed discussion of technological innovations in the television industry is provided in Appendix A.)

Japanese experimentation in television technology was first conducted in the 1930s at Hamamatsu Technical High School (now College) and NHK (Japan Broadcasting Corporation) Research Center. By 1939, when NBC began black-and-white broadcasting in the United States, NHK was publicly demonstrating its successful experiments, and Japanese manufacturers had reached the stage of making experimental television receivers. It was not until after the war, however, that television technology was fully and successfully developed in Japan. In 1949 research at NHK was resumed, and within four years, official broadcasting began in Japan on the U.S. standard.

Because Japan was considerably behind Western countries in technological capabilities in the 1940s and early 1950s, it acquired Western technology from such companies as RCA, EMI in the United Kingdom, and Philips in the Netherlands. Japan acquired access to over four hundred patents, particularly in the areas of component manufacturing techniques. Absorption of foreign technology played a major role in the development of Japan's television industry.

With the advent of color television, Japan repeated its earlier picture of all-out acquisition of foreign black-and-white television technology, including manufacturing expertise. The Japanese emphasized from the beginning a strategy of improving and building upon new but proven technologies rather than investing in basic R&D for technological breakthroughs. Adopting this strategy has allowed Japanese electronics manufacturers to pick an emerging product area and enter it fully confident that component sources, engineering department, production workers, and distribution network are all committed to securing and maintaining a competitive and profitable marketing position. After 1960 the Japanese television industry began to transfer its full capacity into color television and also started to make headway as an exporting industry. In 1976 when the production of color television receivers surpassed 10 million sets, Japan became the world's leading producer. In addition, this growth in the television industry stimulated the development of related components industries even further.

Developments crucial to Japan's competitive success include the skill and alacrity with which Japanese companies incorporated solid-state technology in their receivers, allowing them to assume a technological lead over the U.S. industry; the use of integrated circuits to reduce power consumption and the number of necessary components, combined with automated production and improved quality control, enabling Japanese manufacturers to survive and prosper during the oil embargo and other economic challenges of the mid-1970s; and technical advances in product design and product engineering, facilitating rapid Japanese dominance of the new VTR industry.

Technology Transfers

Technology transfers played a critical role in the development of the Japanese consumer electronics industry and continue to be important.

Transfers of foreign technology have occurred principally at an industry-to-industry level, although the Japanese government has been involved to a significant degree both in regulating the inflow of foreign technology and in acquiring and then disseminating it.

With few exceptions, the Japanese color television manufacturers have acquired foreign technology through licensing and technical aid agreements. Yet at the same time, these firms have been careful to upgrade the technical capabilities of their personnel in order to ensure successful transfers. Until the early 1970s, the Japanese color television firms were primarily interested in transfers that led to an improvement of existing technology rather than new-product or process technology. At an individual firm level and in aggregate, Japan's acquisition strategy was geared toward a gradual but constant expansion of the existing technology base. Only in more recent years has an emphasis on the transfer of new-product or process technology been the rule rather than the exception. In either case, a major motivation in Japanese consumer electronics firms' acquisition of foreign technology has been to reduce internal commitments of time and money to basic and developmental R&D work.

There is little debate that technology transfers were central to Japanese color television firms' growth strategy from the industry's beginnings in the early 1950s to at least the late 1960s. From Sony's 1954 licensing agreement with Western Electric Company for the manufacture and sales of transistors in Japan to Toshiba's 1964 technical tie-up with Ampex for VTR technology, the leading Japanese consumer electronics firms have relied on U.S. firms as a source for next generation basic technology. (See Appendix B for a discussion of the development of the VTR.) Yet although Japanese firms have made a number of specific foreign technology acquisitions that have had a substantial effect on upgrading the technological capability of the industry, more important has been the steady inflow of relatively less-substantial product and process technologies from foreign sources. Japanese firms have not had to rely on one or two critical foreign technologies for their corporate health, a fact that is well expressed in Sanyo's 1972 10K form to the U.S. Security and Exchange Commission: "Although the Company considers that, in the aggregate, its [foreign] patents constitute an asset of some value, it does not believe that any one of them is of such importance that its expiration or loss would materially affect its business."

One way that Japanese firms have maintained the inflow of foreign technology has been through agreements for the exchange of technical expertise with foreign firms. These agreements can be characterized as technological relationships that have afforded the Japanese partner with a means of ensuring constant incremental technology upgrading. In 1952, for example, Matsushita concluded such an agreement with N.V. Philips, and in 1956 the firm entered into similar agreements with the Mallory Corporation and Western Electric Corporation. Similarly RCA has been one of the major sources of technology for Japanese consumer electronics firms and since October 1954 has maintained an engineering laboratory in Tokyo to serve Japanese licensees. This type of technological agreement has allowed the Japanese firms to strengthen their technology base gradually.

The actual amount of foreign technology imported into the Japanese consumer electronics industry during the 1950s and 1960s, and even today, gives a misleading impression. Not all of the licensing agreements in a given year have represented manufacturing technologies new to the Japanese economy as a whole. Seeing competitors adventuring into new product areas or new production processes through licensing agreements, other Japanese firms have quickly sought and concluded similar agreements, more often than not with the same technology sources as that of their competitors. Or when some firms saw their competitors developing new products or processes themselves, they quickly sought to conclude licensing agreements with foreign sources for a similar technology out of the fear that their technological inferiority would cost them a market share in Japan. MITI, too, has actively encouraged the dissemination of specific technologies throughout the consumer electronics industry in order to maintain strong competition in the industry and thus strengthen international competitiveness.

Fierce competition in the consumer electronics industry accounts for the greater than average number of firms obtaining identical technologies from abroad. A recent example of this duplicative acquisition of foreign technology can be seen in the fact that between November 1977, and October 1978, the Japanese Patent Office granted 354 patent approvals in the field of video discs, including 216 for the N.V. Philips system, 99 for the RCA system, and 39 for the AEG-Telefunken system.

Another recent pattern in the purchasing of foreign technology by Japanese consumer electronics firms is illustrated in Mitsubishi's obtaining of an informational license from RCA in July 1979 for that U.S. firm's video-disc player technology. RCA's technology concerns stylus-type video discs; Mitsubishi had already developed optical-type video discs, which employ lasers. Because video disc manufacturers are unsure at this early stage in the product's life cycle of whether optical- or stylus-type models will be the dominant technology, Mitsubishi has effectively hedged its gamble on this new product and ensured itself against any potential licensing infringement actions. As of mid-1979 Mitsubishi was believed to be the sixth Japanese firm to acquire such an informational license from RCA.

At present, foreign technology is still the cheapest and fastest way for Japanese consumer electronics firms to introduce a new product line. New Nippon Electric, for example, recently entered into a licensing agreement with Kloss Video Corporation of Cambridge, Massachusetts, in order to acquire the U.S. firm's technology concerning an enlarged CTV screening system. Similarly the Japanese firm Trio-Kenwood Corporation concluded a November 1979 agreement with N.V. Philips whereby the Japanese firm will be licensed by the Dutch group for production of optical-system video disc players. The Japanese consumer electronics industry's continuing interest in foreign technology can be seen in Toshiba Corporation's establishment of a patent office in Washington, D.C., in July 1979; a primary function of the office is to strengthen Toshiba's technical information activities. Toshiba's establishment of a Washington patent office is indicative of the measures, both legal and illegal, that Japanese firms take to gather needed information. (While unquantifiable and rarely discussed openly, Japanese involvement in industrial espionage has been significant.)

In sum, foreign technology, from both European and U.S. sources, remains an important aspect of Japanese consumer electronics firms' corporate strategy. Technology transfers still represent the most cost-effective way in many cases to acquire a technology. Additionally reliance on technology transfers serves as a means of risk aversion in that the basic R&D and prototype development work is left to foreign organizations to perform. Nevertheless the technology-transfer policy of an individual Japanese firm is conducted in a way that will complement the firm's internal R&D capabilities.

Japanese Response to Technological Change

The growth of the Japanese consumer electronics industry was greatly assisted by the development or acquisition of solid-state devices and new products such as stereos, color television, and VTRs. By entering the market at a critical juncture of these products' life cycle, the Japanese have been able to overcome the advantages of experience and market position held by their international competitors. Moreover, a synergism has developed between the technologies used in the current generation of consumer electronic products, which has allowed the Japanese to move from domination of one product to another.

In the early 1950s, U.S. component makers were moving into a limited production of transistor radios, built as electronics curiosities. The major U.S. radio manufacturers had traditionally built large console and table radios, had major investments in tube radio production facilities, and in most cases were also major producers of tubes. Thus they saw little incentive for pursuing the new technology extensively. The Japanese government and its fledgling electronics industry, however, saw the small transistor radio as a unique opportunity to enter the world market and earn badly needed foreign exchange. The subsequent lead gained by the Japanese in modern radio design has proven decisive, and today there are no major U.S. producers of radios.

Success with transistor radios paved the way for the Japanese challenge to the U.S. television market. It allowed the Japanese to establish a marketing, distribution, and service organization in the United States, and it made Japanese producers the world's leading experts in the mass production of transistorized circuits. Thus in the late 1950s when the technology had advanced to the point where transistorized black-and-white televisions were possible, the Japanese were able to exploit the technology and become a leader in portable black-and-white television.

A key ingredient in these early Japanese successes was the lack of competition from the major U.S. consumer electronic companies. During this period, the U.S. manufacturers were putting most of their R&D money into the development of color television, mostly in superficial model styling changes each year. Also the Japanese products were generally aimed at specialized market segments at the lower end of the price scale. U.S. manufacturers were not particularly interested in these small segments; they tended to distribute their products through a limited number of franchised dealers, a method incompatible with the mass-marketing approach through department stores, drugstores, camera shops, and discount houses used by the Japanese to penetrate U.S. markets.

U.S. makers seriously underestimated the technological consequences of conceding these market segments to Japanese firms. Although the Japanese were importing or licensing from the United States most of the components used in their products, they took the lead in evolving circuit design to take maximum advantage of the new transistor technology. The Japanese rapidly surpassed their competition in descending the learning curve of printed circuit board assembly, the building block of most modern consumer electronics. Finally the demand for electronic components by Japanese manufacturers naturally led to the development of a sophisticated domestic component industry that could compete with their U.S. counterparts both in quality and price.

Another area where the Japanese were gaining advantage over their competitors was in tape recorder technology. Again their initial efforts were directed toward developing mass-production techniques for the manufacture of consistently high-quality products rather than development of proprietary product technology. Moderately priced Japanese magnetic recording equipment, initially based on foreign technology, steadily improved in performance as methods were found for including advanced features and circuits through advanced product design. As in other areas of consumer electronics, the gap between adaptation of foreign technology and original R&D steadily narrowed as the Japanese came to dominate the international marketplace.

These successes culminated in the late 1970s with growing Japanese dominance in the color television and VTR field. Although color television was a natural progression from black-and-white television and production was spurred by very strong domestic demand, the VTR represented a unique Japanese accomplishment. VTR technology, originally invented in the United States as an industrial product, appeared too complex to U.S. firms to be produced at a price affordable by consumers. The Japanese, drawing on their product design expertise in electronic circuits and tape recorders and developing new concepts in recorder technology, succeeded.

The following series of profiles of Japanese firms adds empirical substance to the outline of Japanese product development and competitive strategy. These profiles reveal the alternative corporate strategies pursued by various successful companies and the differences, as well as similarities, among their production and marketing policies.

Sony

Sony Corporation manufactures a wide range of consumer electronic products and certain commercial items such as dictaphones. One-third of company sales are in television receivers. Recent sales of television sets in both Japan and the United States have flattened, while sales of VTR, audio/hi-fi, and business tape recorders have increased. The VTR represented 17 percent of total sales in the quarter ending January 31, 1978.

Sony, much like Honda, was one of the postwar firms that sprouted seemingly from nowhere. Unlike most other Japanese companies, Sony is only moderately leveraged, with a fifty-fifty debt-equity ratio (compared to the more typical eighty-five-fifteen ratio), and has therefore relied more heavily on its own earnings for company growth than upon Japanese banks. Unable to obtain funding in the way large Japanese enterprises with traditional relationships with major banks (such as Hitachi and Matsushita) were able to, Sony developed from its own meager resources to the prominent position it now holds in world markets today. These origins and characteristics undoubtedly have contributed to its innovative leadership in the consumer electronics field.

Sony management is highly concerned about the institutional environment for creativity and makes a purposeful effort to overcome certain Japanese cultural traits that may inhibit individual initiative and boldness of thought. The company policy has been to achieve a narrow but deep specialization in electronics. The development of the tape recorder, magnetic tape, transistor radio and television, the Trinitron color television tube, and the Betamax videotape recorder all represent Sony emphasis on devising new products from within, with a minimal purchase of technology from outside sources. It also connotes a high-risk-taking profile.

The United States accounts for a quarter of all Sony sales, representing its largest television market. The company's presence in the United States dates back to 1960 when it established a distribution and marketing operation for Sony products imported from Japan called Sony Corporation of America (SONAM). The company made a conscious decision from the outset to market under its own brand name and through its own distribution channels in order to establish itself in the major market of the world. Its strategy of developing its own international marketing facilities has permitted Sony to introduce new products to these existing marketing channels in the United States and Europe, even when the Japanese market was not ready for them. By the time the Japanese market is ready for such products, Sony has accumulated sufficient experience to stay ahead of imitators in Japan and elsewhere.

In 1972 Sony began construction of a color television plant north of San Diego, California, which started operation in July 1973. The plant was originally designed for a production capacity of 30,000 color sets per month, with the intent to supply over half of Sony's sales in the United States from San Diego. The plant was, and still is to a large extent, a final assembly operation, using parts and components, especially the more sophisticated, imported from Japan. But vulnerability to import restrictions, coupled with the OMA, has compelled Sony to increase its U.S. parts content of sets assembled in San Diego. The company undertook plant expansion so that it produced 40,000 sets a month in 1980, with a view toward increasing that figure shortly to 50,000. Sony's share of the U.S. market dropped slightly in 1979 to 6.5 percent (it was 6.9 percent in 1978). Following continuous gains even during the recession, the company still had a fifth of the small-set market and was aiming at a 10 percent U.S. share by 1980.

Sony has responded to market adversities with a three-pronged strategy. One tactic is to refranchise dealers in an attempt to hold down transshipping and price slashing. This tactic has been accompanied by limited promotional sales and a restructuring of the U.S. operation into three companies along product and distribution lines. These three changes are accompanied by a greater degree of control from Sony headquarters in Japan. Sony also revamped its product line, introducing new models during the second quarter of 1980.

Revamping the product line necessitates R&D, for which Sony outspends its competitors. Projection television (the big-screen type) was reduced in price due to cost savings through design changes. Features of larger sets, such as all-electronic tuning and velocity modulation, will be extended to the entire line. A vertical integral reference (VIR) semiconductor chip is expected to be introduced in some sets. A new chassis introduced in May 1980 emphasizes ease of repair. After the back of the set is removed, only two screws stand between serviceman and chassis, which can be manipulated independently of the set while circuits are still operable; printed circuit boards may be removed and replaced with no soldering.

Sony is marketing several products in Japan, all of which may be introduced in the United States. Trinitron II, with a thirty-inch screen, is the largest direct-view color television in the world. Sony's carry-along set, which is battery powered, may be introduced in the United States as part of a drive to introduce some specialty products for department stores, as well as other specialty products. These specialty products will presumably be those sold only to better department stores. A Betamax VTR unit with a new feature adapted from audio discs will be introduced as a super hi-fi audio recorder.

Reversing its long-standing policy of marketing its products exclusively under its own brand name, Sony is licensing several companies worldwide to sell its home VTR, the Betamax, under their own brand names. This break with tradition was necessitated by the intense competition with Matsushita's Video Home System (VHS) for world market shares, as well as for establishment of the Betamax over the VHS system as the industry standard. With competition intensifying, Sony now plans to lengthen its two-hour cassette to compete with the VHS four-hour recorder. Sony's cassettes are smaller than Matsushita's, an aspect in which Sony considers itself to have the advantage. The company has invested $38 million in an Alabama plant to manufacture blank Betamax tapes and cassette shells. These, as well as the VTR, are also targeted for export to Europe. VTR sales have moved from 7 to 17 percent of Sony's total sales in the past three years, and the sale of tapes has outstripped all projections.

Another highlight in recent sales has been the U-Matic, a VTR for commercial use. Sony attributes its leadership in development of VTR, and its status as the only manufacturer of both VTR and blank tape, to the evolution of its late 1940s work on the tape recorder and on magnetic tape. The ability to build on past technologies for new products has given Sony a unique position and a competitive advantage in both tape and VTR sales. Other VTR manufacturers must purchase Betamax tape. Product evolution was a major factor also in Sony's early development of transistorized television technology from transistor radios.

Matsushita

Matsushita Electric Industrial Company, Ltd., is the largest manufacturer of electronics products in the world. Roughly half of its sales are in consumer electronics (television, hi-fi, radio and VTR, and electronic components). Matsushita has fifty manufacturing departments in Japan and twenty-nine overseas, in addition to twenty-seven sales operations overseas.

The company has grown by spinning off profitable product groups and making them subsidiary companies. Export markets have comprised an average of a quarter of Matsushita's sales and have played a strategic role in the company's growth.

Matsushita is one of the two most highly integrated electronics firms in the world (Philips, the Dutch manufacturer, is the other). The company makes 90 percent of its own television components, with 85 percent of all television manufacture automated. Matsushita designed and built its own automated insertion and quality-control machines, which it sells to Sony and other manufacturers worldwide.

Matsushita's debt-equity ratio is more similar to that of U.S. firms than the ratio of most Japanese firms, roughly one-to-one rather than three- or four- to one. The company has recently added to equity through a further stock offering. Profit expectations of management and stockholders are captured by the dictum, "Product, not profit, is the goal." Retained cash held in tax-free reserves is used for product development and refinement of the manufacturing process. Matsushita's average annual budget for R&D—3.6 percent of sales—is higher than the average U.S. expenditure.

Matsushita's primary response to lowered profitability and to an adverse economic environment with which it has had to deal in the past few years is development of new products with higher value added. The company is committed to developing its own products and has an R&D center for each product group. The company is frequently prepared to take initial losses on a product while marketing initiatives establish market demand. Given increased restrictions on Japanese television exports to the United States and tougher competition from Taiwanese and South Korean manufacturers, Matsushita's top management has decided that mass marketing and production is no longer an appropriate growth strategy.

Specialty products for specific markets will be a Matsushita thrust in competition with other leading manufacturers. An example is a wireless record player that transmits sound through FM waves, requiring no connection to speakers. Other products in the conceptual stage include wrist-watch television receivers and facsimile machines for home use to replace newspapers. The company's concern with long-term growth has made it a leader in new-product development and a leading holder of patents in Japan and overseas.

Although new products have been responsible for increased sales, intensive efforts at value engineering have been behind reduced costs. These efforts have the effect of moving a product down the learning curve as the number of parts are decreased and the volume of production rises and have also assisted Matsushita in pulling through the recession. For example, parts count in radio cassettes have been reduced by 30 percent and the number of required components in Matsushita's television picture tube was reduced by 40 percent over the number in the 1976 model.

Matsushita's newest product, the video disc, is made entirely with standard components and can be assembled in any of its overseas plants, as sources of raw materials or import controls may dictate. Panasonic (a brand name) color television consoles for the U.S. market are being manufactured in Canada and Korea, as well as in Japan. In keeping with a national imperative to move manufacture closer to the source of raw materials and to avoid the high cost of land in Japan, Matsushita increased the number of manufacturing operations it has overseas to twenty-nine in the past few years.

Matsushita's sales efforts have intensified. Going directly to dealers and customers around the world, Matsushita tailors product innovations to consumer requests. The VTR is made in a low-price and a long-playing model, after price and short playing time were isolated as barriers to sales. Each product group and model is linked to a very specific segment of the market; small-size refrigerators for the growing singles market and for hotel rooms, oven toasters, for young married couples, and various models of battery-powered televisions directed to the youth market for use outdoors have been recent marketing successes in Japan.

Export markets, which constitute approximately one-third of total annual sales, are similarly segmented and are considered crucial to the company. Quick movement down the price and learning curve enabled Matsushita to gain on Sony's early lead in the VTR market. In 1977 the company showed gains in VTR sales in North America, color television sales in the Middle East, hi-fi equipment sales in Europe, and refrigerator sales in Southeast Asia. The average annual growth rate for exports has been 17.5 percent over the past five years, outstripping overall sales growth, despite an appreciating yen and increasing raw materials prices.

The purchase of Motorola's television assets in 1974 gave Matsushita a base of manufacturing in the United States. Motorola, with losses of over $20 million and realizing the amount of R&D necessary to create the next product generations in television, offered its television operations to Matsushita. Despite heavy expenditures in redesign and retooling, Quasar (a trade name Matsushita has retained from the most popular Motorola television model) had dropped in market share from the 1973 level of 8 percent to 5.9 percent in 1975 and to 5 percent in 1979. Matsushita has replaced all Motorola models and will now use a new chassis in Quasar sets. The new "super module" contains 75 percent of the previous model's circuitry and is replaceable in three minutes should the set need repair. The new module, with integrated circuits, reduces the number of parts to 550 from 640, cuts the wiring to 125 from 250 feet, and cuts power consumption to 120 watts from 170. All of this engineering work has been done by Matsushita in Japan, leaving terminated Motorola engineers applying for aid from the U.S. government in the form of adjustment assistance.

Despite these modest design changes and automation of the Quasar plant to reduce unit production costs further (85 percent of insertion is done by machine), Quasar has yet to show a profit for its new parent. The latest Matsushita attempt to revive Quasar sales is the introduction of the VTR and the microwave oven into the Quasar line to achieve wider name recognition. In order to increase its competitive edge in VTRs over the noncompatible Sony Betamax system, Matsushita has also licensed the VTR unit for sale by RCA, Magnavox, GE, and GTE Sylvania. Panasonic also sells VTRs.

Matsushita has redesigned the VTR each year for three years. Both component quality and set performance have been improved. Materials research yielded heavier video heads with longer wear, as well as new magnetic materials permitting high-density recording. The new direct-drive cylinder is a product of the firm's motor technology laboratory, and mechanical and operational improvements provide easier tape loading. New features, in response to consumer demand, include longer playing time and the addition of a digital clock and timer.

In 1977 Matsushita's founder, Konosuke Matsushita, broke with industry precedent by elevating a relatively young man, Toshihiko Yamashita, to the post of company president. Recruitment from the lower ranks served as a signal to young engineers that the seniority system would not stand in the way of improved performance. Other Japanese firms have since emulated Matsushita's move in a response to the tougher economic outlook. Although the consensus style of management encouraging vigorous and critical evaluation from below still prevails, management now recognizes that the company's rapid growth has interfered with communication between top management and lower echelons and with the traditional autonomy of manufacturing departments. The sales division too often worked without interchange with other divisions. Manufacturing divisions were too loosely controlled, leaving smaller units almost ignored. The new president has instituted monthly management meetings to let middle-management know what top management is thinking, while trimming head office staff. The newly appointed Yamashita toured all fifty domestic manufacturing departments himself.

Matsushita stays at the outer limits of the state of the art in electronics by participating in government-sponsored research, applying the findings of its various research facilities to electronics products, and responding directly to consumer demands by redesigning products. Rigorous quality-control testing is done not only by engineers but by women employed at the factory on a part-time basis.

Quality control is simplified because the company's own production machinery is so fully involved at every stage. The company uses its own products not only in the factory where components and insertion and testing machines are largely Matsushita designed and built, but also in the design of packaging in which sets are shipped. The firm also follows up on consumer products as they are marketed through communication with distributors. Customers are queried through distributors as to what degree they are satisfied with their product. To dispel the bias company engineers might have toward their own products, consumers are employed part-time to test products themselves.

Hitachi

Hitachi, Ltd., was founded in 1910, with the goal of providing a Japanese alternative to dependence on foreign technology in production of electrical equipment. The firm's repair shop made several types of five-horsepower motors without outside assistance and then began manufacturing them. After World War II, Hitachi expanded its generating equipment facility and diversified in light of lower demand and increased competition worldwide. Hitachi today is one of the largest companies in the world. Its products include heavy electrical machinery such as generators, atomic power facilities, semiconductors, transistors, and consumer electronic products. The company operates thirty-eight subsidiaries, including both overseas sales firms and manufacturing units.

Hitachi is heavily capitalized and is a conservative firm with a financial structure and marketing orientation in the traditional Japanese mode, unlike Sony's and Matsushita's. The company shows the three- or four- to one debt-equity ratio typical of most other Japanese firms. It has tax-deferred income, which is reserved for R&D expenditures. Company management expects to finance further growth through joint ventures overseas, as well as through sale of technology. R&D expenditures typically are about 3 percent of annual sales. There are thirteen laboratories covering research in all product groups.

Declining profitability in the early 1970s and following the oil crisis was attributed to high fixed costs for maintenance of plant and for labor, excess capacity, increased materials costs, and yen appreciation. During this period sales increased overall, but both color set and tube sales were down. The company went into television manufacture in 1969 because of the prospect of increased domestic and export markets, but Hitachi managers no longer view color television as a growth item; the audio line therefore is being strengthened.

The consumer-products division, which includes appliances, accounted for about 22 percent of sales in 1979. Export sales are necessary so that Hitachi can maintain volume and support its heavy capital investment. Hitachi exports have climbed for the past several years. Company management would like to achieve even higher volumes of export but sees this as difficult, except in terms of joint ventures and sales of technology overseas.

Recently Hitachi and General Electric planned to form a joint company in the United States called General Television of America (GTA), which would produce a million sets a year and employ 6,300 persons. Technology, including engineering design and quality control techniques, would have been provided in large part by Hitachi. Color tubes for the original equipment manufacturer market would also have been manufactured. The joint venture was stopped by the U.S. Justice Department's Anti-trust Division. Hitachi also explored and dropped plans for a plant in northeast England. Invited by the U.K. Ministry of Industry, Hitachi was pushed out by the objections of the British television industry's management and labor who pointed to the current excess capacity in television manufacturing in the country. But Hitachi has recently entered into a joint venture in Singapore for the manufacture of television.

Hitachi's management operates on the premise that R&D is the driving force behind progress. The company does basic research, production research, and research into application technology. Both to cut costs and to meet the shift in demand of the Japanese market to quality sets, Hitachi has progressively reduced the number of parts in its chassis. The company makes 70 to 80 percent of its components and its own testing and packaging machines, all of which enhance quality-control efforts. A notable innovation is Hitachi's robot, developed in 1975. The working model has tactile sense and is capable of performing high-precision positioning of parts, although it has not yet been used in television assembly operations. The company considers itself a leader in this type of pattern-recognition technology.

Recent innovations in television technology include all-electronic (varactor) tuning and the first fault-proof, self-convergence tubes. The 110° deflection tubes dispense completely with previously necessary circuitry. Hitachi is also working on the video disc and now markets its own VTR commercially. Liquid crystal, or flat-panel, television is being developed, and a new motor for audio turntables is on the market. Hitachi also is working on a portable television the size of a book.

Hitachi had about 10 percent overemployment during the recession and could not lay off personnel because it is a large company functioning under the lifetime-employment system. Since the recession of the mid-1970s, there has been a decrease in total employment every year, probably signaling a freeze on new hiring. The company has instituted labor-management discussions directed at making optimum use of labor. Some of the extra employees were shifted to sales-and-service subsidiaries. Small suppliers to Hitachi did what laying off of employees had to be done. Those components Hitachi does not make itself are supplied by these small supplier firms, and they are the ones that made large cutbacks during the recession. Automation and rationalization of design and production of component suppliers' operations, under Hitachi direction, obviated the need to rehire workers previously laid off by these smaller firms.

Hitachi's sales suffer from conservative marketing and design styles. It projects an image in both the United States and Japan of reliability but lacks any dimension of excitement or novelty. In keeping with its conservative policies in marketing is Hitachi's reliance on Japanese managers for its overseas subsidiaries. Products exported to the United States are rarely redesigned for American tastes. Hitachi had hoped that its joint venture with GE would enable incorporation of American preferences and marketing feedback into set design. Establishment of a U.S. production site is expected to fulfill that rule.

Sanyo

Sanyo Electric Co., Ltd., manufactures consumer electronic products, electric household appliances, commercial electrical equipment, and gas and oil appliances. Sixty percent of the company's sales are in consumer electronics, including audio products, calculators, and emergency broadcasting systems. The oil crisis and consequent decreased demand affected the company, as did import quotas. Sanyo is structured with the heavy debt typical of most other Japanese firms and relies heavily on export sales to pay interest costs.

The company was established after World War II as a manufacturer of bicycle lamp generators and began television production in 1957. Sanyo's management philosophy, like that of most other Japanese firms, is based on technological innovation aimed at providing inexpensive quality products tailored to consumer demands.

Sanyo operates nine overseas companies, the latest being Sanyo Manufacturing Corporation (SMC), which was established in early 1976, with the acquisition of Warwick, a U.S. set manufacturer in Forrest City, Arkansas. Supplying Sears, Roebuck and Co., Warwick, faced with crippling losses, had asked Sanyo to provide technical assistance against a mounting failure rate for its televisions. Sanyo, anticipating higher U.S. tariffs or quotas on television imports, countered with a purchase offer and is now the majority owner. The company began by buying most television parts from Japan, but Sanyo is increasing the U.S. content of its sets to 50 percent. Sears remains the major purchaser.

Due to record sales, Sanyo is expanding the former Warwick plant in Arkansas. When Sanyo came in, automation of assembly was stepped up. The company now produces in one wing what used to be produced in four. Production has risen from 424 sets a day to 2,800, and the 1,000 workers laid off in 1976 have been rehired. Rigorous quality controls were instituted so that if a screw falls out of a set during a test, the error can be traced back to the worker responsible for the screw. Sanyo has struck off in a different direction from its competitors in its management of its U.S. facility. A team of three Americans and three Japanese runs the plant. Adopting the lifetime employment system to the fullest extent possible, Sanyo has stated that no workers will be laid off. In the end Sanyo hopes to instill in its U.S. work force the same loyalty and dedication found at its domestic facilities.

Sanyo is a leader in modularization and parts reduction. Its television sets use a single printed circuit board rather than multiple printed circuits. In one year, parts were cut from 1,300 to 120, work time was halved, and set life increased. Quality control is done by teams outside of the regular chain of command. Sanyo has adopted its zero-defects policy in its Arkansas facility, reducing service calls on sets to almost none. Like Matsushita, Sanyo does its own package design and testing. It also makes 80 percent of its own components. Sanyo is actively developing its video disc player and manufactures its own micron precision cylinder heads for tape systems. But although it independently developed a VTR system, it has yielded to Sony's VTR system for standardization reasons.

4

Government's Role in Industry Development

Three basic factors contributed to the birth and early growth of Japanese television manufacturing: the reinforcing support of the government-sponsored television broadcasting system, the technical contribution of foreign (mostly U.S.) technology, and the additional purchasing power of U.S. personnel stationed in the Far East.

Japanese television broadcasting began in 1953 with the February inauguration of Tokyo Television Station, a public station run by the government's Japan Broadcasting Corporation (NHK); in August Nippon Television Network Corporation (NTV), a commercial station, started operations. Although NHK had adequate technological capabilities in the broadcasting field, the government corporation's purchase of state-of-the-art equipment from U.S. firms allowed it to upgrade its technological base quickly and efficiently. In a short time, the NHK research laboratory was developing its own broadcasting technology based on this technology inflow and distributing production orders for equipment to the small, fledgling Japanese electronics industry. NTV, the commercial station, also relied initially on U.S. expertise, which was transferred through a U.S. government grant in the form of technological aid and facilities. In 1951 Matsutaro Shoriki, a former president of a leading Japanese newspaper, had approached U.S. Senator Carl Mundt after learning of his advocacy of establishing international television facilities for Voice of America broadcasts; Mundt maintained that it was then possible to popularize television in Japan at a cost of only $4.6 million. Shoriki proposed establishment of NTV with this funding to Mundt, who agreed to this proposal and won congressional support for the plan.

After World War II the Japanese electronics industry, along with the rest of the economy, was in shambles. Because the Japanese government could not promote the electronics industry through defense contracts, the industry had to develop around consumer goods. Yet although the start of television broadcasting in 1953 by the government certainly acted as the major stimulus to the industry's growth, it cannot be said that the government, in introducing such broadcasting, attached greater importance to the consideration of developing an indigenous television industry than to a desire to start broadcasting for social, cultural, and political rebuilding. When broadcasting began in Japan, domestic receiver production was limited, and most television sets were imported.

Yet it is obvious that by late 1953, the Japanese government was intent on developing a domestic television industry and using this to develop a broader electronics industry. In November 1953, the Ministry of International Trade and Industry announced a policy of extending assistance for the development of Japan's television receiver production. As a result, television imports were restricted from the end of that year. Additionally the government began to promote the utilization of foreign (mostly U.S.) technology by domestic manufacturers. Government-conducted R&D work on television, done primarily at NHK, was made available to industry. Through these and other measures, domestic manufacturers from about 1955 on were able to make dramatic production increases. By 1957 domestic plants had achieved an output level of 613,000 units. From 1957 to 1958, output doubled to 1.2 million units, and from 1958 to 1959 it more than doubled to 2.8 million units. The U.S. market became an important sales outlet when the domestic market could not absorb these domestic production increases.

The presence of a large number of U.S. servicemen highly exploitable and highly liquid consumers, stationed in Japan after World War II and during the Korean War served as a significant market for the Japanese television manufacturers. The Korean War additionally stimulated a domestic economic boom, which completed the postwar reconstruction of Japan's economy and further strengthened an already sizable domestic market for consumer products such as television.

After the war, Japanese firms, both small enterprises like Sony and larger firms like Matsushita, began a limited but rapidly expanding production of such items as radios and tape recorders (indigenous tape recorder production began as early as 1949). In many cases the U.S. electronic products, both consumer and non consumer, which accompanied the U.S. servicemen stationed in Japan, were reverse engineered by the Japanese firms for reproducible copies. In this way initial international technological capabilities were developed by the Japanese consumer electronics industry. With the introduction of television broadcasting, this reverse engineering was performed on RCA and Zenith sets by Japanese firms. In part to overcome the then-prevalent image of poor Japanese quality, the Japanese television manufacturers emphasized high quality and upgraded the component quality of the American models they copied. Many of the early top-of-the-line Japanese sets, for example, were built with very high-quality sound systems; these systems were later removed when it became obvious that the average Japanese consumer did not care about such high quality.

From the earliest postwar days to the present, the Japanese consumer electronics industry has been characterized by an extremely competitive and fluid structure. In 1948, for example, there were as many as eighty radio manufacturers (the predecessors of television set makers), but the number declined to eighteen in 1950 as a result of the 1949 recession. Many of these surviving radio manufacturers, together with relatively small companies such as Sanyo that emerged during the radio boom of 1951-1952 (created by the commencement of private radio stations), moved to take up the production of monochrome television sets when television broadcasting began in Japan. The large majority of these firms entered into licensing agreements with such Western companies as RCA, Westinghouse, Philips, and EMI. In fact with the commencement of television broadcasting in Japan in 1952, as many as thirty-three Japanese firms quickly acquired licenses. But a market law, designed to promote the survival of the fittest, soon eliminated many of them, and by 1961 98.1 percent of the television market was controlled by the top ten firms (52.2 percent by the top five and 19.6 percent by the leader). Thus at the outset Japan's television industry was—and still is—fiercely competitive.

Japanese mass production of color television began in 1964 in anticipation of a large consumer demand stimulated by the Olympic Games to be held that year in Tokyo. Yet domestic demand for color television sets did not develop as rapidly as the Japanese firms hoped. As with black-and-white sets earlier, the U.S. market provided an outlet for the increasing volumes of production. And again, with the introduction and growth of color television production, government assistance and foreign technology played key roles.

Overview of Business-Government Relations

During its years of development from the early 1950s to the late 1960s, the Japanese consumer electronics industry received an indeterminant amount of direct and indirect government aid. The indirect government assistance was found generally in the broader mandates of the Japanese government designed to restructure the postwar economy. Direct government assistance was distinguished by targeted government efforts (financial or government R&D work) in critical areas that contributed to the dynamic growth of the consumer electronics industry.

Throughout the 1950-1970 period, MITI's industrial policies were characterized by a judicious manipulation of the industrial environment. Starting in 1952, foreign firms' access to the Japanese market was severely limited by MITI's restrictions on foreign direct investments in Japan, as well as on the importation of goods and technologies to Japan (significant movement toward trade liberalization began in 1968). Behind this protective shield erected around Japan, private firms were encouraged to compete with one another in order to demonstrate their vigor. When weaker competitors were shaken out of the competitive process, MITI rewarded the surviving firms with further financial and technological incentives.

Since the late 1960s, the Japanese consumer electronics industry has not been receiving substantial amounts of government aid. Through a combination of external and internal pressures, government efforts to define the broad outlines of the Japanese economy have become less and less vigorous. Direct governmental assistance to the consumer electronics industry has been sharply reduced as other glamor industries move to the fore. Thus since the late 1960s, the computer equipment industry has eclipsed consumer electronics as the industry whose present development the government believes will be most beneficial to the national economy and, therefore deserving of government assistance.

Another factor that has served to reduce the government's role in the consumer electronics industry has been the fact that the industry has developed into a strong one. It is highly competitive in international markets and therefore no longer needs much in the way of governmental assistance. The promotion of exports is a fundamental policy of the government, and past promotion measures in the consumer electronics industry have done well enough to lead to a sizable flow of consumer electronics exports, independent of government assistance. What direct government assistance does occur still is targeted toward critical areas, usually at the developmental stage of new products, and is primarily concerned with increasing the export competitiveness of the industry.

An examination of the various Japanese consumer electronics firms reveals a host of factors contributing to their success, only one of which is government support. Production efficiencies, reduced costs through economies of scale, an embracing of the learning-curve principle, high-powered and innovative marketing, and self-generated R&D breakthroughs are only some of the characteristics of Japanese consumer electronics firms that have contributed to the strength of the industry. Such characteristics are further enhanced by the traditional Japanese system of compromise and consensus.

Japanese economic development has been a case study in government-business cooperation, with the government often out in front promoting the interests of business. As one observer put it, " 'GE stands for GE and to hell with the United States. . . . But Hitachi is primarily and fundamentally Japan.' That makes all the difference."[1] Combined with a national commitment in the post-World War II era to catch up with the West, this cooperative approach has produced a very healthy climate for doing business—so healthy, in fact, that there has been a backlash in recent years, with consumers petitioning the government to look after their interests, as well as those of producers.

The most tangible evidence of this harmonious government-business relationship is the institutions designed to promote it. Among these are the Japan Electronic Industry Development Association (JEIDA) and the Electronic Industry Deliberation Council. JEIDA, which is composed of over twenty-five chief executive officers of Japanese electronics firms, was established in 1958 in response to the Provisional Measures Law of 1957. JEIDA's stated objective is to promote R&D and industrial rationalization, the latter a common goal of MITI, which often has worked behind the scenes to increase the international competitiveness of industries by seeking to restructure them. Primarily concerned with consumer electronics in the 1960s, JEIDA has since shifted its focus to the computer industry.

The Electronics Industry Deliberation Council, which the Japanese government directed to be established within MITI, brings together government economists, physicists and engineers, industry representatives, and outside experts (a total of forty members) to discuss problems, research topics, and policy proposals. The council, part of MITI's Electronic Industry Section, serves as a forum to harmonize views; its position thus represents a formal guidance to MITI policy.

More important perhaps for the sake of government-business cooperation has been the government's commitment to industry growth. As part of this commitment, MITI in the past has organized and financed research consortia. In 1966, for example, MITI coordinated and helped finance an R&D program aimed at commercial application of solid-state technology. In the mid-1970s, the government was instrumental in establishing a computer research consortium among the larger, leading electronics firms.

When it acceded to the OMA with the U.S. government in 1977, the Japanese government was placed at cross-purposes with the consumer electronics industry. Nonetheless MITI resumed its traditional role of structuring the Japanese response by taking responsibility for allocating the designated annual quota among the Japanese exporters. The OMA with the United States is not a unique action on the part of the Japanese government; under pressure from European governments MITI first restricted color television and tape-recorder export prices in 1972 and then negotiated a voluntary export agreement in January 1974.

Another area in which the government has taken on an adversary role vis-à-vis the industry—quality control—has come about in response to consumer pressure. When presented with consumer displeasure, MITI on occasion has called in the relevant manufacturers and asked them to correct the problems. They invariably do. It is in keeping with the tenor of government-business relations in Japan that such matters are handled informally.

The Provisional Measures Laws[a]

The three successive provisional measures laws (1957-1971, 1971-1978, and 1978-present) have been the most-visible and perhaps most-important pieces

---

[a]The material in this section is based on translation of legislation under discussion. Translations were provided by the Japanese Division of the Library of Congress.

of Japanese government legislation in regard to the consumer electronics industry. The objective of these laws has been the development and strengthening of the industry. Yet these laws have only indicated specific means of assisting industry and specific areas to direct this assistance; they have not committed the government to offer that assistance. Further, amounts of government funding have not been specified in the laws. In short, it is not possible to determine the extent to which these laws have been implemented and thus the degree to which they have assisted the consumer electronics industry.

The Machinery Temporary Measures Act was authorized in 1956 and was a precursor to the provisional measures laws. Not restricted to electronics, the act provided various Japanese industries with direct grants and long-term, low-interest loans in order to stimulate acquisition of foreign technology and investment in R&D.

The Provisional Measures Law for the Promotion of the Specified Electronic and Machine Industry, enacted in 1957 and effective until the end of March 1971, was the first of the provisional measures laws. It provided financial assistance for the development of targeted growth products in the electronics field and offered extra depreciation allowances to Japanese firms based on increased exports, as well as tax exemptions for expenditures to develop overseas markets.

The Provisional Measures Law for the Promotion of the Electronic Industry, which succeeded the 1957 to 1971 law and was effective from 1971 to 1978, designated three categories of electronics equipment and components to be potential recipients of distinct forms of promotional assistance (each equipment or component category specified fifteen to twenty items). The first category of electronics equipment and components was for those "necessitating the promotion of more research and development," in light of the fact that Japanese technology in these areas was behind foreign technologies. In this category the only item directly related to consumer electronics was the high-capacity picture tube. Financial assistance under the title of "subsidies for research and development of important technologies" was designated for first-category-type equipment.

The second category was for those electronics equipment and components necessitating the start of industrial production or an increase in the volume of production." The only consumer electronics item in this category was the electronic VTR. The Japan Development Bank was to offer loans for the commercialization of new technology for equipment and components in this category.

The third category was for those items "necessitating promotion of modernization of production facilities," and the color VTR was the only consumer electronics entry. Third-category-type equipment and components qualified for a "special depreciation system for machinery for modernization purposes" based on the Law for the Promotion of Modernization of Enterprises, as well as special financing from the Japan Development Bank.

Each of the three categories contained a description of the steps that MITI believed would be necessary to achieve the goals of additional R&D production start-up or increase, or rationalization of production. This included matters such as the number and types of production machines required and an estimate of the total amount of money that would be necessary to complete these steps. These estimates did not constitute in any way a commitment that such funds or machinery be provided to manufacturers by the Japanese government, either directly or indirectly. These were statements of certain goals and estimates of the means required to achieve these goals.

The 1978 update of the 1971 to 1978 law was the Provisional Measures Law for the Promotion of the Specific Machinery and Information Industry. This law is primarily directed toward the assistance of Japan's computer industry; the only consumer electronics item specified in any of the three categories for this 1978 update is magnetic cartridges in the second category.

Technical and Market Development

Most R&D in Japan is done by private enterprise. Yet the government does participate in R&D work in specific areas, usually those involving either basic research or new-product conception. Government R&D work has played a significant role in contributing to the dynamic growth of the industry.

Most government R&D work with a direct bearing on the Japanese color television industry is conducted at the Japan Broadcasting Corporation, or NHK, laboratories. Yet other government-controlled laboratories have engaged in R&D work that has either direct or indirect application to color television specifically and consumer electronics in general. KDD Research and Development Laboratory, for example, through its work in the communications field has assisted the consumer electronics industry in digital electronics and satellite-to-home television systems. Nippon Telegraph and Telephone (NTT), in cooperation with consumer electronics firms, has taken part in the development of home facsimilies.

Although much of NHK's work focuses on improving broadcasting techniques, these laboratories do offer technical assistance and guidance to electronics manufacturers in accordance with their requests. The NHK labs were reorganized in 1965 when the Broadcasting Science Research Laboratories branched off from the Technical Research Laboratories. The former conducts the more-basic research, such as studies on vision and hearing, as well as solid-state properties. The latter is involved in a wider range of activities, including improvements of current broadcasting techniques and development of future broadcast systems and techniques. Between them the laboratories employ four hundred people, including about forty engaged in research. About 6.5 billion yen (U.S. $30.9 million) was spent by NHK on all forms of R&D in 1978.

The Technical Research Labs maintain seven research groups, at least five of which appear to have some relevance to the consumer electronics industry: the New Broadcasting System Research Group, the Radio Frequency and Satellite Broadcasting Research Group, the Recording Techniques and Memory Devices Research Group, the Image Devices Research Group, and the Advanced Television System Research Group.

The New Broadcasting System Research Group has been involved in, among other activities, developing a still-picture broadcasting system, capable of conveying simultaneously a number of informational or educational programs composed of color still pictures, with or without sound, on a conventional television channel. The Advanced Television System Research Group has performed studies on new, high-definition television systems. The Recording Techniques and Memory Devices Research Group has conducted a variety of research activities relating to magnetic video recording, including a high-density video recording system for reducing the quantity of recording tape, a portable eight-head VTR system using one-inch wide tape, and electron beam recording of picture and sound, used for compact storage of broadcasting programs. Although developed for broadcast use, these devices can be spun off into consumer applications. (In 1974 this research group began work on digital audio and digital video technology, which is being continued at present.) NHK also has developed a compact cassette VTR for educational use. The Image Devices Research Group studies various kinds of camera tubes, picture tubes, and solid-state image devices.

The Radio Frequency and Satellite Broadcasting Research Group has been involved in such work as satellite broadcasting system design, including development of a low-cost, low-noise receiver of satellite signals for home use. The NHK believes that such receivers are essential for the diffusion of satellite broadcasting and is developing a high-sensitivity model for the purpose. These receivers will be far less expensive than present conventional microwave circuit elements. Field trials of satellite broadcasting began in July 1978 and were conducted by NHK using Mitsubishi's direct-to-home receivers.

NHK is not the only government agency engaged in research relevant to the consumer electronics industry. Another, the Kansai Electronic Industry Development Center (a regional laboratory with national funding), coordinated a project begun in April 1966 to develop black-and-white sets and color television receivers utilizing integrated circuits for as many functions as possible. This project, organized with the financial assistance of MITI, brought together five major Japanese manufacturers (including Matsushita, Mitsubishi, and Sanyo), seven parts makers, four universities, and two institutes. A prototype black-and-white set was completed in 1967 and a color set in 1968. Another government agency, the Japan Research Development Corporation (JRDC), financed entirely by the government, promotes the exploitation of scientific research in Japan on an industrial level. Among the projects JRDC has worked on are solid-state devices and designs and processes for components manufacture. Of the nearly eight hundred inventions submitted to JRDC since its inception, one hundred have been accepted for commissioning. The success rate, as measured by technical success in industrial application, is quite high.

MITI itself has conducted large-scale projects attempting to develop voice-controlled technology. And Densoken, the Electric Technology Research Center of MITI's Agency of Industrial Science and Technology, has developed video disc technology. By mid-1978 four leading Japanese electronic firms, including Mitsubishi and Hitachi, had launched plans for pilot production of a video disc based on this new technology.

In sum, the Japanese government has played and continues to play an important role in the stimulation of R&D work in specific areas related to consumer electronics with well-targeted but limited funding. It is difficult to compare Japanese and American government assistance to their respective electronics industries due, in part, to differences in funding for armament research. Estimates for Japanese government R&D funding vary from below 10 percent to as high as forty percent, with some observers arguing that Japanese firms, particularly large ones with dominant market position, fund virtually all of their own R&D efforts.

Closely related to the government's R&D activity is its efforts to create and stimulate markets for new products. One of the government's key mechanisms in this effort has been the anticipatory development, promotion, operation, and licensing of broadcasting or transmitting facilities appropriate to new products under development by consumer electronics firms. Coupled in some cases with government purchasing orders for these new products, this government activity has served to create a domestic market for industry to exploit. In this market, industry can refine these new-generation products for export in anticipation of similar market developments overseas.

Government efforts to develop consumer electronics markets began in the early 1950s with the promotion of private radio and television broadcasting, work that led directly to the growth of domestic consumer electronics industry. Later government promotion of color broadcasting facilities helped create the color television market. In late 1978 the government began licensing domestic private networks to air multiplex-stereo broadcasting, and all public broadcasting companies have begun such broadcasting. As a result, consumers who have purchased the newly developed multiplex-stereo television equipment are able to receive an ever-increasing range of stereo or multilanguage broadcasts. The Japanese manufacturers of multiplex products, in turn, have an immediate outlet for these new products.

Nippon Telegraph and Telephone Public Corporation's (NTT) active promotion of the development and propagation of the home facsimile device (which may be used to receive any type of data or information) is another example of government-led market development. In 1972 NTT opened its ordinary telephone circuit to facsimile use. Up to that time, a limitation in existing transmission facilities was the major roadblock to dissemination of facsimiles. With this problem removed, business enterprises began readily to adopt facsimiles as an office tool. Both NTT and the manufacturers envision that the facsimile (either analog or digital) will be a major consumer electronics product in the 1980s and 1990s. Production of the facsimile by consumer electronics firms expanded at an annual rate of 30 to 70 percent in terms of value in the years following NTT's move. NTT also opened a new facsimile communication network in 1981. Through subscription rates charged for access to either this new network or the regular telephone network, NTT anticipates sizable returns on what it believes will be a potentially huge market for the home facsimile. Aside from realizing a substantial cash flow from this service, NTT will also contribute to the development of the Japanese consumer electronics firms' capabilities to commercialize the home facsimile successfully. With this objective, NTT recently finished performance tests of the third (and final) trial models furnished by six manufacturers, including Matsushita, Hitachi, and Toshiba. Experimental production orders have been placed by NTT to promote commercialization of the product.

The confluence of government-industry interests in this example should be noted. Part of NTT's motivation for the development of the home facsimile was that it promises to be a service with a substantial market among NTT's telephone service subscribers and should result in sizable returns to NTT. Thus NTT's activity in the home facsimile field cannot be viewed solely in terms of a calculated move by the Japanese government to give Japanese industry an initial advantage over foreign competitors in a market that could prove substantial over time.

Satellite broadcasting is another area in which market development efforts are under way. NHK's research on home receivers for satellite broadcasting, now being produced by Mitsubishi, promises to help open up this market to commercialization. Another more-involved method of market creation is currently taking place in the community of Higashi-Ikoma, where 158 households are participating in a government-sponsored test project of Hi-Ovis (highly interactive optical-visual information system) a two-way audiovisual communications system.

Taking a much different tack for market development, MITI, through its active interest, has given new life to a broad program for increasing exports of industrial plants that was conceived by the Japanese government several years ago but allowed to lay dormant. MITI has determined that television sets will prove increasingly difficult to export to foreign markets; establishment of overseas production bases is seen as a way of avoiding importing countries' concerns over too high a level of Japanese imports yet still enabling Japanese industry to exploit these markets. In July 1979 MITI established the Plant Export Basic Policy Committee, the salient features of which are a committee of experts made up of representatives from government and industry, which will promote exports of plants on a consortium basis with foreign companies; investigation teams, which will be dispatched to offer postexport consulting for plants exported to less developed countries; and strengthened capabilities for the gathering of information on risks in various countries. MITI's new program aims at promoting the formation of consortia with foreign firms and securing the cooperation of these firms' governments; it thus hopes to confer regularly with similar committees formed in the U.S. and Europe and then get them to set up consortia for the projects upon which they decide. Again television is one of the first products MITI will attempt to act on. MITI believes that the establishment of an international consortium system would greatly facilitate exports of industrial plants to the Middle East, Southeast Asia, and Latin America. Japanese efforts to establish this system constitute an attempt to extend the principle of institutional harmonization from the domestic to the international economic sphere.

Financial and Trade Dimensions

Since the early 1950s, Japanese consumer electronics firms have witnessed a variety of government involvements concerning financial and trade aspects of their industry. These involvements have included both direct legislation and indirect measures.

Tariffs

A comparison of U.S. and Japanese tariffs applied to color television shows that, starting in 1965, U.S. MFN (most-favored-nation) tariffs were considerably lower than equivalent Japanese tariffs until at least 1972, and perhaps beyond. (See table 4-1.) The Japanese general rate of 30 percent was significantly higher than equivalent U.S. rates from 1965 to 1970. A big change came in 1971 when the Japanese general rate fell to 7.5 percent (still slightly above the U.S. rate of 6 percent). A temporary Japanese rate of 5 percent began in 1972, and this was lowered to 4 percent in 1973 and 1974 (lower than the U.S. rate of 5 percent). According to the Japanese law covering tariffs, the temporary rate should have taken precedence over the general rate (7.5 percent) because it was lower.

In 1970 the Japanese government enacted the Customs Temporary Measures Law to provide duty-free treatment for the foreign content in Japanese television sets and certain electronic components imported from abroad. This law facilitated imports from areas with low labor costs, notably in the Far East. (The law is comparable to items 806.30 and 807.00 of the Tariff Schedules of the United States.)

Nontariff Barriers

In the 1960s and early 1970s, nontariff barriers (NTBs) were the primary means by which the Japanese government protected the domestic consumer electronics market. Promient among these NTBs were quotas and controls on capital and foreign exchange. As Japan's consumer electronics industry developed to where it no longer needed such protection and as Japan moved to meet Organization for Economic Cooperation and Development and International Monetary Fund commitments, these restrictive measures were eased and then abolished.

Table 4-1
Comparisons of U.S. and Japanese Tariffs on Color Television Receivers, 1965-1974
(percent)

Year	United States Most-Favored Nation	Japan General	Temporary
1965	10 ad valorem	30.0	
1968	9 ad valorem	30.0	
1969	8 ad valorem	30.0	
1970	7 ad valorem	30.0	
1971	6 ad valorem	7.5	
1972	5 ad valorem	7.5	
1973	5 ad valorem	7.5	4
1974	5 ad valorem	7.5	4

Note: There have been no changes in tarrifs in either the United States or Japan since 1974.

The extent of protection given to the industry by these NTBs is not clear. Some observers claim that protection of other Japanese growth industries, like steel and automobiles, was much greater by comparison; U.S. producers, according to this analysis, simply "missed the boat" in penetrating the less-protected consumer electronics market. Others, however, and Zenith in particular, claim these NTBs were used to keep them out of the Japanese market.

In any case, U.S. producers did not penetrate the Japanese market during its growth years. Instead in order to generate residual earnings, they chose to license their technology to Japanese entities. (At the same time, a few U.S. firms, such as General Electric, built European plants to get behind tariff walls there.) As a result, they narrowed the technology gap between themselves and foreign producers and locked their U.S.-based plants into producing almost exclusively for the domestic market. At the same time, the U.S. government tolerated Japanese (and European) protectionism due to the strategic exigencies of postwar reconstruction.

Capital Controls

Capital controls prohibited direct foreign investments in black-and-white and color television production. Partial liberalization of allowable investment levels (up to 50 percent) in black-and-white facilities was granted in July 1967. Full liberalization (100 percent) for both black-and-white and color television production was not granted until March 1969.

Three major reasons for capital controls can be identified: the fear that profit remittances would cause balance-of-payments problems, worry about the monopoly potential of larger foreign firms, and an overriding desire to prevent foreign control of higher-technological industries.

Foreign Exchange Controls

Under provisions of the Japanese Foreign Exchange and Foreign Trade Law (law 228, December 1949), foreign exchange controls gave MITI the power to allocate foreign exchange for imports. Upon attaining article 8 status (in part, the requirement not to impose restrictions on international currency transactions) in the IMF on April 1, 1964, Japan abolished these controls.

According to internal Zenith documents, television receivers with screen size up to fourteen inches were covered by the so-called Exchange Fund Allocation (EFA) system. Under this system, according to Zenith, MITI was supposed to issue fund allocation certificates automatically and with no amount of limitations. Zenith claims that in 1962-1963, MITI refused to allocate foreign exchange to its importing distributors because Zenith's products were so popular.

Given the interest of several of Japan's most prestigious firms in developing consumer electronics products as export industries and the high priority given to imports of raw materials and foodstuffs, importers of finished electronic goods could not have expected to receive a very sympathetic hearing from MITI. Moreover the high priority given to imports of raw materials and advanced industrial equipment and the virtual prohibition of consumer goods imports ensured that the latter would be costly.

Quotas

Foreign exchange controls were replaced by import approval, or quota, systems, in April 1964. The three quota systems were the import quota (IQ), the automatic import quota (AIQ), and automatic approval (AA). Of these systems, only the IQ system was designed to limit the quantity of imports. Under the terms of the IQ system, MITI retained the right to approve or disapprove applications for import quota certificates and to limit the size of the quota. The AIQ system was designed as a way station for import items removed from the IQ system. The main purpose of the system was to obtain statistical information on import trends following liberalization. MITI was supposed to grant unrestricted import quota certificates within forty-eight hours, and imports under the AA system were to be free from all quantitative limitations.

Zenith, in internal documents, claims the AIQ system was not automatic because MITI could deny the quota application or establish a very low quota. Zenith also believes the approval systems hindered its ability to provide after-sales servicing and maintenance.

Color television and its parts were both on the AIQ system in 1969, and color televisions were switched to AA status in August 1971; parts followed in October 1971. The AIQ system was abolished in February 1972 and the AA system in December 1972.

Controls on Foreign Technology Purchases

MITI played an important role in the importation and diffusion of foreign technology. MITI's powers in this area derive from the Foreign Investment

Act of 1950, which required governmental approval of all transactions involving remittances in a foreign currency.

MITI's aims in controlling foreign-technology purchases were essentially threefold: to keep practice and restrictions on use to a minimum, to give priority to technologies that promised to benefit the economy as a whole, and to diffuse technologies throughout industries to prevent monopolies.

Much has been said about MITI's intervention, threatened or real, in ongoing negotiations for foreign technology and how this was used to keep prices down. Rumors abounded that government authorities insisted on seemingly endless adjustments in the terms of technology contracts as a condition of approval. This convinced many foreign sellers that government and business were conspiring to improve the bargaining position of the Japanese purchasers. It is worth noting that royalty rates paid by Japanese firms averaged less than 4 percent prior to liberalization in 1968 and have since exceeded 5 percent. This, however, could be due less to liberalization than to the increasing unwillingness of foreign licensees to provide the Japanese with technology at such inexpensive rates.

MITI also objected to technological agreements that limited exports, which individual firms may have been willing to enter into in return for lower royalty rates. Nonetheless in 1971 three-fourths of all technology agreements had export restrictions.

Before 1968 MITI gave priority to technology for intermediate goods, such as chemicals and machine tools, and suppressed the domestic demand for foreign technology in such areas as consumer goods. After trade liberalization, the total number of contracts for foreign consumer electronics technology shot upward, indicating that MITI's controls in this regard had some effect. Nonetheless from 1960 through 1965, imports of technology became more oriented toward consumer goods and potential exports, and after that for improvements on technologies already imported. When a technique was introduced for one firm, MITI made an effort to see that it was available to others.

Price Fixing

Whether the Japanese government has been involved in price fixing has been a very controversial subject. Certainly MITI has a history of organizing recession cartels and stabilizing prices to prevent excessive competition from driving firms out of business. But that is not the same as organizing or even sanctioning unfair prices in general.

Those, like Zenith, who accuse the Japanese of dumping blame MITI's protectionist measures of the 1960s for permitting domestic producers, free of foreign competition, to collude in keeping prices artificially high. There is also evidence that MITI directed the Japanese consumer electronics firms to enter into agreements with respect to minimum prices and other matters concerning exports to the United States. Such agreements apparently existed from 1972 until 1973, a period of time that roughly coincides with that in which Japanese television companies achieved extraordinary growth in the American market at the expense of established American companies. MITI claims to have initiated these agreements in order to prevent Japanese exports from causing unnecessary disruptions in the national economies of Japan's trading partners. The continued difficulties in the American consumer electronics industry, however, raised doubts about whether MITI was concerned about the U.S. economy or Japanese firms' success.

The *Journal of the Electronics Industry* argues that although Japanese exporters "on the advice of the Government, adopted the lowest standard export price system for television sets to be exported to the U.S.," the exporters guaranteed that export quotations would be higher than the fair price unofficially indicated by the [U.S.] Treasury Department. Furthermore Japanese exporters "made the effort to follow that procedure," but the Treasury Department changed the fair-price calculation method in mid-1970, "and quoted a new fair price that was quite unfavorable to Japan."[2] As a result, the Japanese were found guilty of dumping in September 1970.

Clearly the Japanese government was engaged in setting prices for export; it is not clear, however, that these prices were unfair. Moreover no evidence has been put forward to prove that the government aided in or acquiesced to domestic price fixing. Finally, U.S. protests that the setting of minimum export prices violates U.S. antitrust laws simply point up the difference in American and Japanese business practices: what is antitrust here is commonplace there.

Another possible indication of price-fixing was the 1970 nationwide boycott in Japan of high-priced color televisions. The boycott was directed primarily at Matsushita because of that firm's artifically high prices, though it may have involved other sellers of particularly expensive models as well. Price fixing in this situation would only be implied if the action were directed at a number of major firms. The boycott apparently ended with MITI's directing home appliance makers in November 1970 to cut their indicated prices by 15 percent.

Finally those analysts who emphasize the dynamic nature of the Japanese economy claim that export prices are the result not of collusion but rather of intense competition in the domestic market. Internal price competition among companies in Japan has typically been as intense as in the United States, and in several industries Japanese earnings have depended more heavily on exports.

Government Subsidies and Financial Assistance

The overall financial environment in Japan is conducive to industrial growth and is supported by broad government policies. Yet direct government subsidies or financial assistance to any given industry segment are difficult to detect and appear to be modest amounts at most. Various government measures have provided financial incentives for exporting, R&D efforts, and investment in capital equipment. The extent of government assistance to the consumer electronics industry has decreased over time. Government subsidies and financial assistance have often been cited as major factors in the high performance of Japanese industry. Yet on the whole more important has been the financial leveraging for R&D and capital equipment investment that Japanese firms have been able to obtain from the country's banking establishment.

The relatively low and sporadic level of direct governmental financial assistance nevertheless has been critical to the dynamic growth of the consumer electronics industry. Government funding has been provided at critical points of product development. The Japanese government has concentrated its financial assistance activities on the high-risk areas (from a business standpoint), leaving the commercialization and production technology development to private industry. Through direct subsidies or grants to firms or research organizations, purchase order for undeveloped products, and its own R&D work, the Japanese government keeps its direct financial assistance to industry well targeted on new-product development. These new products may then lead to industry exploitation of new domestic and export markets.

The Japanese government is able to make a little funding go a long way to enhance Japanese industry's international competitiveness by concentration almost exclusively on commercial-oriented funding. On the other hand, the U.S. government, which funds a significantly greater percentage of industry R&D work than does the Japanese government, directs its funding activities primarily to defense projects that in some cases have spin-off commercial application.

Financial assistance in the form of tax incentives and export rebates to the consumer electronics industry has contributed to new-product development and commercialization, as well as reinforced export drives in the industry. Yet the government trend has been away from extending these financial mechanisms to the consumer electronics industry.

The most significant legislation aimed at providing incentives for R&D commercialization and modernization in consumer electronics dates back to the Machinery Temporary Measures Act of 1956, which provided industry with direct grants and long-term, low-interest loans. Subsequently the 1957 to 1971 Provisional Measures Law for the Promotion of Specified Electronic Industry also specified certain consumer electronics areas as being appropriate for loans for R&D, commercialization, or modernization, although to a lesser degree than its predecessors. The Provisional Measures Law for the Promotion of the Specific Machinery and Information Industry, enacted in 1978, is aimed primarily at the computer industry and provides for limited assistance to the consumer electronics industry.

The leveraging of debt by Japanese corporations, reinforced by government-backed liberal lending policies, has been an extremely important contributor to the risk affinities of many (but not all) Japanese consumer electronics firms that might otherwise be more conservative in their commitments to technological change. This leveraging by Japanese color television firms has been promoted by the Japanese government through its Economic Planning Agency, which, in its annual economic survey, indicates to the nation's commercial banks which industries should be given first priority for loans. In the past, the Japanese government's efforts to assist the consumer electronics industry by making large amounts of capital available from banks has served as a critical comparative advantage in an increasingly capital-intensive industry.

Incentives for Export

The Japanese government has always been preoccupied with exports. Most of the targeted growth industries were expected to, and did, export on a large scale. Consequently many observers have attempted to explain Japan's phenomenal growth rates in terms of export-led growth, and some have stressed the role of government export incentives.

The first legislation designed specifically to promote the consumer electronics industry, the Provisional Measures Law for the Promotion of the Specified Electronic and Machine Industry (1957), contained two export incentives: extra depreciation allowances based on increased exports and tax exemptions for expenditures to develop overseas markets. Consumer electronics firms were also eligible for production finance loans granted at concessionary rates by MITI, the Ministry of Finance, and the Export-Import Bank of Japan, if the firms tied the loans to an expansion of export capability.

To the extent that consumer electronics firms produced for export prior to 1957 (the extent was minimal), they benefited from export credits, guarantees, and tax incentives applied indiscriminately by the government—even exporters under voluntary export restraint benefited from these aids. Up to 1971 the consumer electronics firms (especially television manufacturers) received a form of short-term export credit from banks at preferential rates. But in August 1971 the government-run Bank of Japan led the way in discontinuing the practice of rediscounting preshipment export bills at preferential rates of interest. At the same time, the bank also discontinued preferential rates of interest for loans against foreign exchange assets.

Notes

1. Philip M. Boffey, "Japan (III); Industrial Research Struggles to Close the 'Gap.' " *Science,* 167, no. 16 (January 1970):267.
2. *Journal of the Electronics Industry* (November 1979):54-66.

Part III
Japanese Competition in the U.S. Color-Television Market

The U.S. Market and Japanese U.S.-Based Production

Demand and Market Shares

The American public has purchased more than a quarter of a billion television receivers (approximately 85 million have been color sets) since regularly scheduled television broadcasting was resumed after World War II. From 6,000 sets in 1946, annual U.S. sales increased to more than 7 million in 1950 and then fluctuated between 5 million and just under 8 million annually for the next ten years. With the color television boom, sales of all television sets to dealers have exceeded 11 million units annually every year since 1964, peaking in 1973 when nearly 17.5 million sets were produced or imported.

The demand for color television receivers rose from 6.2 million units in 1968 to 10.1 million units in 1973. Following the 1974 recession, demand fell to 6.2 million units in 1975 and recovered to over 9 million color sets by 1977. Between 1973 and 1975, there was a 30 percent decline in sales value of color television receivers, from $3.1 billion to $2 billion. Yet not surprisingly, the steady growth in U.S. production of color televisions, which was given a substantial boost by the influx of Japanese producers, has been directly paralleled by growth in domestic sales; 1979 sales in the U.S. market were more than 31 percent higher than 1978 sales and more than 48 percent higher than 1977 sales.

Of all the color television sets sold in the United States in model year 1979, a little over one-half (55 percent) were supplied by the major U.S. manufacturers (Zenith, RCA, General Electric, Admiral, and GTE-Sylvania and GTE-Philco), while over one-quarter (26.75 percent) of the U.S. market was captured by the brand-name products of foreign-owned manufacturers (Magnavox, Sony, Matsushita, Sanyo, Sharp, Hitachi, Mitsubishi, and Toshiba). Foreign-owned companies also acted as the principal suppliers to the private-brand retailers (Sears, Montgomery Ward, and J.C. Penny) and captured 11.5 percent of the 1979 market. (Table 5–1 provides a historical breakdown of U.S. market shares.)

From 1970 to 1979 the major U.S. color television manufacturers witnessed a decline in market share from 72.8 percent to 55 percent. This decline can be attributed to the increase in Japanese imports at the expense of U.S.-firm market shares and to a less obvious factor: the purchase of Magnavox by N.V. Philips of the Netherlands in 1975 and Quasar/Motorola

Table 5-1
Market Share of Color Television Sets Sold in United States, 1970-1979
(percent)

Manufacturer	1970	1971	1972	1973	1974	1975	1976	1977	1978	1979
Zenith	20.6	19.9	19.1	22.5	23.75	24.0	23.0	22.0	21.15	20.5
RCA	22.8	20.8	20.5	20.3	20.5	19.0	20.0	20.0	20.0	21.0
Sears	7.1	8.7	8.5	7.8	7.5	8.7	9.0	9.0	8.65	7.9
Magnavox (Philips after 1974)	9.5	10.0	8.9	8.0	6.75	6.6	6.5	7.0	7.0	7.0
Sony	—	—	3.3	4.0	5.0	5.8	7.0	7.5	7.0	6.5
General Electric	4.6	5.2	5.3	6.0	6.0	6.2	5.5	6.0	6.6	6.9
Quasar (Matsushita after 1974)	5.7	5.2	7.0	8.0	6.75	5.9	5.0	5.0	5.4	5.0
Sylvania (GTE)	4.6	4.3	4.5	5.0	5.0	4.4	4.5	4.0	3.6	3.9
Panasonic (Matsushita)	—	—	—	—	—	2.3	2.5	3.0	3.0	2.2
Admiral (left the industry in 1979)	5.0	4.3	4.2	3.5	3.5	3.0	3.5	2.5	2.5	1.5
Sanyo	—	—	—	—	—	—	—	—	2.0	2.0
Ward	—	—	—	—	—	—	—	2.0	2.0	2.1
Sharp	—	—	—	—	—	—	—	2.0	2.0	1.5
Hitachi	—	—	—	—	—	—	—	—	1.75	1.55
Penney	—	—	—	—	—	—	—	—	1.6	1.5
Philco (GTE after 1975)	—	—	2.7	—	—	2.0	1.5	1.5	1.55	1.2
MGA (Mitsubishi)	—	—	—	—	—	—	—	—	1.0	1.0
Other brands	20.1	21.6	16.0	14.9	15.25	12.1	12.0	8.5	3.2	6.75

Source: DEWIT, Inc., compilation.

by Matsushita in 1975 represented the loss of over 12 percent U.S. market shares. The switch of private-brand retailers like Sears and Montgomery Ward in the mid-1970s from U.S. brands to Japanese brands has also counted for a significant, but hidden loss of U.S. firms' market share; since 1977 these outlets have accounted for over 10 percent of the U.S. color television market. More significantly the percentage of U.S. value content in color television sets has declined dramatically over time. From an estimated 62.2 percent U.S. value content in 1972, color television sets sold in the United States by U.S.-owned manufacturers in 1978 contained approximately 30.3 percent U.S. content.

In regard to the question of U.S. value content, it is notable that virtually all of the U.S. manufacturers' chassis subassemblies are imported. In color picture tubes, which are predominantly assembled in the United States, approximately 12 percent of the value added is of foreign origin, represented specifically in the television gun and flyback transformer. Thus of the 40 to 45 percent value added for a completed set represented in the color picture tube, an average 12 percent is of overseas origin.

American companies manufactured virtually all of the television receivers sold in the country from 1948 (when black-and-white television sets were first introduced into the United States) until 1962, when Japanese imports accounted for about 2 percent of black-and-white sales. In 1967 the first imported color television receivers were introduced to the U.S. market, and within three years, 17 percent of this market was supplied from abroad (and about 50 percent for black-and-white). During the six-year period from 1969 through 1974, imported color television receivers held a constant 15 to 17 percent share of the U.S. market.

Beginning in late 1975, the U.S. industry began experiencing greatly accelerated competition from imports, particularly from Japanese firms. In the second half of 1975, color television imports rose to over 22 percent of the U.S. market and concluded the year at 19.5 percent. The most dramatic jump in imports occurred in 1976, with 34.6 percent of color televisions sold in the United States originating abroad. The aggregate value of U.S. imports of color television receivers in 1976 was $522 million, representing almost 3 million units. Although color television imports from January through June 1977 ran nearly 34 percent above the first half of 1976, by year end 1977, the share of the U.S. market supplied from abroad had dropped to 27 percent. By 1979 only 9.2 percent of U.S. consumption was accounted for by imports, yet this statistic is deceptive because it does not reveal the continued steady increase in market share by the Japanese firms producing in the United States; in 1979 over 40 percent of the U.S. market had been captured by foreign firms.

The loss of U.S. market shares is attributable to a considerable degree to misjudgments on the part of U.S. management concerning the U.S. color television market. Despite growing market demand for compact models, as late as 1975 Zenith and RCA persisted in their emphasis upon console model production (over 50 percent). They did this despite the much greater income elasticity of demand for compacts over consoles (six times) and the growing preference among high-income groups in the United States for Japanese compacts.[1] These high-income groups and their growing preference for Japanese products contributed to the subsequent success of Japanese-made VTRs.

The rising market share in the United States that is supplied by foreign firms is but one indicator of the present state of the U.S. industry. Financial problems have forced several U.S. television manufacturers into mergers or acquisitions, and some U.S. firms in the industry, such as Rockwell International's Admiral division, have been forced out of business altogether. In 1968 there were eighteen manufacturers of television receivers in the United States; by 1980 there were thirteen, nine of them foreign owned. In addition, an increasing portion of the U.S. manufacturing operations are being shifted offshore to low-wage economies and shipped back to the United States for final assembly.

The movement offshore has been reinforced by a seemingly chronic state of underutilization of plant capacity in the United States by color television manufacturers. In fact, in the years from 1971 to 1977, U.S. television receiver assembly plants were operated at levels of capacity that were between 5 and 15 percentage points lower than the levels at which all U.S. manufacturing plants as a group were operated. Although capacity utilization in the industry increased from the 1976 level of 58.8 percent to 70 percent in 1979, this increase was due primarily to the acquisition of existing U.S. facilities by Japanese producers. Yet in part because of the offshore movement, the U.S. television industry has suffered substantial unemployment and underemployment since 1975. In 1971 total direct employment in the U.S. industry was 42,920 workers; in 1979 the work force had been reduced to 26,190, a 38 percent decrease.

Japanese Investment in the United States

In August 1972 Sony became the first Japanese firm to begin production in the United States. To alleviate U.S. demand pressure on overstrained Japanese facilities caused by an extremely successful penetration of the U.S. market, Sony constructed a five-line final assembly plant outside San Diego, California. Sony's San Diego plant makes extensive use of parts and components imported from Japan, especially the more-sophisticated ones. Vulnerability to import restrictions, however, coupled with the OMA, has compelled Sony to increase its U.S. parts content of sets assembled in San Diego, and the company has undertaken plant expansion so that it now produces 40,000 sets (versus an initial capacity of 30,000 sets) a month, with a view toward increasing that figure shortly to 50,000. In August 1977 Sony purchased and shipped to San Diego most of the tube production equipment from a former East Coast Westinghouse picture tube plant.

Matsushita was the second Japanese firm to invest in manufacturing in the United States, this time through acquisition of Motorola's color television division for over $100 million. Since the early 1960s, Matsushita has marketed its Japanese-made products in the United States and Canada through a distributorship and under the brand name of Panasonic. The acquisition was largely intended to quiet U.S. criticism of Japanese exports to the United States. Motorola's brand name of Quasar was retained for Matsushita color television made in the United States, and Matsushita acquired Motorola's three plants in Illinois. Two of the plants have been phased out of operation, but the one in Franklin Park has been expanded and given a new, entirely automated assembly line to produce totally redesigned Motorola sets.

The third Japanese investor in U.S. color television manufacture took the same approach as did Matsushita. In December 1976, the Sanyo Electric Company acquired Warwick's color television plant in Forrest City, Arkansas, having purchased the Whirlpool Corporation's controlling interest in the then-floundering enterprise. Sears, which held 25 percent equity in Warwick, retained its share of the operation, and Sanyo has bought all but about 2 percent of the outstanding interest in public hands. The Forrest City plant, as it was with Warwick, is basically involved in the assembly of solid-state sets, receiving circuit boards and other parts from feeder plants in Japan. Sanyo has been very concerned with raising quality-control standards, and new sophisticated testing equipment, as well as a complete television-signal-generating system, has been installed. Virtually all production is sold to Sears for private-brand retailing. Whirlpool sustained losses of $12 million in the last two years that it controlled Warwick, but Sanyo was reporting a profit within a year (although it has suffered slight losses since then).

Mitsubishi Electric Corporation and Toshiba are more recent Japanese television investors, having opened assembly operations in Irvine, California, and Lebanon, Tennessee, respectively. In spring 1977, Mitsubishi leased facilities in California and began assembly of nineteen-inch complete color kits imported from Japan, which were then sold through its U.S. marketing subsidiary, Melco Sales. Once the OMA was in effect, the plant was forced to stop operation because the kits fell under the quota for complete sets. Melco reopened the plant in February 1978 and began assembly of nineteen-inch color portable sets and twenty-five-inch color console sets for sale under its own MGA brand, using parts from both the United States and Japan. Capacity of the plant now totals five hundred sets a day, but depending upon the sales level, Melco may expand the U.S. plant's monthly capacity to ten thousand sets. In the meantime, the company is working to increase the U.S. content of its sets, which currently represents about half of the cost and is composed of the speaker, cabinet, transformer, other electronic components, and labor. The main chassis and picture tube are still manufactured in Japan.

The Toshiba facility near Nashville, which began assembly of nineteen-inch color portables in July 1978, entailed an initial investment of slightly over $5 million out of a total projected cost of about $8.3 million. The company has estimated that about half of the cost of materials in its American-made sets represents parts and components procured in the United States. Toshiba America imports printed circuit board assemblies and certain other chassis components from plants in Japan but would like to find a U.S. supplier.

Hitachi's proposed joint venture with General Electric, blocked by the U.S. Justice Department in late 1978, would have provided this Japanese enterprise with a major production presence in the United States. Because this joint venture was not allowed by the U.S. government, Hitachi sought its own production base in the United States. In 1979 the Japanese firm selected Compton, California, as its site for U.S. manufacture. In that same year Sharp also decided to establish a U.S. production presence in Memphis, Tennessee.

The U.S. economy can take little comfort in the reverse flow of investments into the United States despite positive short-term balance-of-payment and employment effects. The OMA triggered a large-scale movement of Japanese capital investment into the United States, yet the result is that the U.S. economy is becoming the supplier of low-skill labor for assembly and the low-technology range of components (cabinets and glass for picture tubes). The sophisticated range of products continues to be imported from Japan (chassis assemblies, including electronic components and tuners). Similarly the production function for high value-added products and products that promise strong growth potential is retained in Japan.

The long-term implication of this trend is that Japanese design-engineering capabilities will be further enhanced, and U.S. capabilities will continue to decline. U.S. industrial employment in the color television industry is being increasingly relegated to the positions of assembler and cabinetmaker because the major components (except for picture tubes, at least for the time being) to a large extent are now manufactured abroad and to an increasing degree designed and engineered abroad, either in U.S.-firm offshore sites or in Japan-based plants.

Determining Considerations for
U.S.-Based Production

Underlying the Japanese decision to establish U.S. production facilities was the recognition of the importance of the U.S. market, despite the problems of duplicating facilities abroad and price and exchange fluctuations that complicate overseas operations. This commitment to the U.S. market is reinforced by a belief that U.S. market share can be increased, implicitly at the expense of U.S. firms. Thus Japanese firms' U.S.-based production facilities will be complemented with expanded field service and sales networks in the United States. Further, the Japanese color television manufacturers plan for increasing automation in their overall operations and act accordingly, in contrast to the continued disinclination or inability on the part of U.S. firms to move in that direction. The Japanese firms believe that this fact supports a move onshore because high U.S. labor costs can be circumvented by increased automation. Japanese firms also see the dual strategy of volume production and product line broadening in the United States as contributing to successful ventures. Finally the Japanese have faith that their organizational and managerial skills can be translated into strong U.S. presences.

Between 1972 and 1980, seven Japanese color television manufacturers established production facilities in America (see table 5-2). Underlying this trend toward onshore production by Japanese firms are several factors: Japanese fear of and reaction to a growing U.S. protectionist sentiment (as manifested in the OMA and dumping charges); the appreciation of the yen vis-a-vis the U.S. dollar; the progressive narrowing of cost differentials between color televisions produced in the United States and in Japan; and the need to develop quicker response capabilities for a major market.

Table 5-2
Japanese Onshore Production Facilities

Firm	Location	Date of Production Start	1979 Production Capacity Range
Hitachi	Compton, Calif.	Late 1979	36,000- 50,000
Matsushita	Franklin Park, Ill.	1974	700,000-800,000
Mitsubishi	Irvine, Calif.	1978	150,000-180,000
Sanyo	Forrest City, Ark.	1976	700,000-900,000
Sharp	Memphis, Tenn.	1979	100,000-120,000
Sony	San Diego, Calif.	1972	500,000-700,000
Toshiba	Lebanon, Tenn.	1979	300,000-400,000

Source: DEWIT, Inc., compilation.

Defensive Reaction to U.S.
Protectionist Measures

As the major Japanese consumer electronics manufacturers' color television exports to the United States began to show substantial increases during the first half of the 1970s, a strong protectionist sentiment began to build among the U.S. consumer electronics industry, with Zenith taking the lead. This sentiment led to the U.S. industry's seeking legal and financial redress through a variety of import-relief petitions and litigation designed to invoke the imposition of U.S. import restrictions on the Japanese firms.

A major complaint brought against the Japanese television manufacturers was filed by the Committee for the Preservation of American Color Television (COMPACT), a lobbying group composed of five U.S. companies and eleven labor organizations. In 1976 the group petitioned the International Trade Commission (ITC) for an import-relief investigation, based on the charge that television receivers were being imported in such increased quantities as to be a substantial cause of serious injury to the U.S. industry. Although the ITC agreed and recommended higher tariffs, President Ford instead opted for an OMA negotiated with the Japanese government.

On July 1, 1977, an OMA between the two governments went into effect covering color television receivers for a three-year period. Under the terms of the agreement, imports of complete color television receivers from Japan were limited to 1.56 million units and incomplete receiver imports were restricted to 190,000 units annually. The effect of this OMA on the Japanese firms' strategy for penetration of the U.S. market can be seen in the fact that Japanese color television receiver imports reached 2.5 million units in 1976, the year preceding the OMA, and thus entailed a sharp reduction in imports for the Japanese firms. The terms of the OMA required a 40 percent decrease in Japanese imports.

Although the 1977 OMA must have caused those major Japanese color television manufacturers not already producing onshore to consider this move seriously, they were still, briefly, afforded an alternative. This OMA permitted Japanese (as well as U.S.) manufacturers to export color television sets freely to the United States from Taiwan and Korea. This option was taken away in 1978 when first Taiwan and then Korea were forced to negotiate similar marketing agreements with the United States.

This restriction of Korean and Taiwanese export channels left Singapore as the only immediate offshore production base available to the Japanese firms. Because the Japanese consumer electronics firms also expected Singapore to be drawn into an OMA, they were left with the choice of either making a fresh move into some new offshore production center or accepting the fact that from then on sales of color television sets in the United States might have to be supplied chiefly by manufacturing subsidiaries inside the country. As a result, Mitsubishi and Toshiba established U.S. production sites in 1978, with Hitachi and Sharp following suit in 1979.

The establishment of onshore production facilities seemed to be a relatively attractive alternative to a loss of sales volume in the U.S. due to OMA import restrictions. The importance of OMAs in serving as a major impetus to move onshore by these four firms should not be underestimated, but several other factors and considerations also contributed to this movement. That three Japanese color television manufacturers were already onshore before the 1977 OMA went into effect indicates in part the importance of these other factors.

The other major set of protectionist measures that influenced Japanese consumer electronics firms toward the establishment of onshore production facilities involved legal measures initiated by U.S. consumer electronics manufacturers. These measures included charges raised against the Japanese manufacturers of dumping, unfair import competition, and antitrust activities. Dumping allegations began in the late 1960s. Thus the onshore movement of Japanese firms, both before and after the OMA, was in some degree an attempt to soften criticism of aggressive behavior in the marketplace. This criticism is part of what the Japanese have seen as a growing protectionism in the United States that might have led to an effective closing of a major market.

Appreciation in the Value of the Yen

A significant factor in causing Japanese color television manufacturers to consider producing in the United States has been a continuous increase in the value of the yen relative to the U.S. dollar. As early as 1971 Sony Corporation was examining the effect of an appreciating yen in regard to a decision to establish production facilities in the United States.

An appreciating yen influenced Japanese firms toward onshore production for three reasons: color television price advantages between sets produced in Japan for export and U.S.-produced sets were being eroded, repatriation of earnings from export sales in the United States became less attractive, and requirements for capital investment in U.S. assembly or manufacturing facilities were less expensive when translated into their yen equivalents.

Narrowing of Production Cost Differentials

Although the yen's appreciation contributed to a reduction in the price advantage enjoyed by Japanese color television exports over sets manufactured in the United States, this advantage was eroding anyway throughout the late 1970s due to a narrowing of production costs between sets made in Japan and those made in the United States. Significant increases to Japan of the costs of energy, raw materials, and world transportation have made Japanese firms more receptive to the idea of establishing U.S. onshore production facilities.

Need for Quicker Market Response Capability

Because the U.S. market has represented the largest nondomestic market for Japanese color television manufacturers and plays a critical role in their global strategies, these firms increasingly have felt the need to develop quicker response capabilities to changes in this market. Establishment of onshore assembly and marketing operations has been viewed by Japanese firms as providing a better ability to gauge and react to changes in demand and consumer tastes in the U.S. market than might otherwise be possible if production was exclusively sited thousands of miles away. Yet Japanese firms have been much more hesitant to expand U.S. procurement of components and parts because of the dramatic differences they perceive between American and Japanese suppliers, particularly in terms of quality-control standards and responsiveness to demands for changes in design.

By establishing assembly sites in the United States, Japanese color television producers are more able to adjust quickly their product flows to meet the demand in the U.S. market. The closer proximity of a production facility to the market it services eases inventory problems, and local production, at least in theory, should allow for more-frequent and rapid adjustments between market needs and the assembly line. Nevertheless Sony Corporation of America, for example, has not always been able to take full advantage of this quickened adjustment capability because of communication problems with its parent firm in Tokyo.

An additional benefit of onshore production for Japanese consumer electronics firms lies in these firms' improved capability to assess market trends. This is true for both the gauging of consumer preferences for new or existing products and the monitoring of consumer complaints about products.

Response Patterns of Individual Firms

The seven Japanese color television manufacturers that have set up U.S. production facilities have done so for a combination of factors. The weight of each factor in the corporate decision-making process of each firm may have differed to some degree. The timing of each firm's decision to move onshore provides a clue as to the relative weight of these factors in that decision. Sony's movement onshore in 1971 suggests concern about the appreciating yen and about developing a quicker response capability for a major market. Toshiba's movement onshore in 1978 would seem to be more a direct result of rising U.S. protectionist measures, particularly the OMA. Yet although a host of factors no doubt influenced Hitachi's recent move onshore, the U.S. Department of Justice denial of a merger between Hitachi and General Electric was the more immediate catalyst.

The overriding concern of all the Japanese firms that have moved onshore has been to secure and expand market share in their most significant nondomestic market. Three of the four major factors influencing the movement onshore have been coercive in a sense. Rising U.S. protectionism, the appreciating yen, and narrowing cost differentials are factors seriously considered in the boardrooms of Japanese color television firms and over which the board of directors have no direct control. These factors most likely precipitated a movement onshore before the Japanese firms would have liked, with the possible exception of Sony. Yet direct exports from Asia were becoming increasingly unfeasible, and the Japanese color television manufacturers have been quick to accept this new reality of doing business in the U.S. market.

The seven Japanese color television manufacturers currently operating production facilities in the United States appear committed to these U.S. operations in the short to medium term. These firms' plants have been adding production and assembly lines either to increase output or broaden the onshore product line. The longer-term commitment of these firms to onshore manufacture will, of course, be determined by these operations' profitability. The key factors that will reinforce the Japanese firms' commitment to onshore production or cause them to expand their presence will be a continued narrowing of production costs between U.S.- and Japanese-sited plants; continued U.S. protectionist sentiment; the success of marketing color televisons with new features and advanced new products, such as the VTR or video disc, in the United States; and the ability to capture U.S. market share from U.S. color television manufacturers due to aggressive business practices and/or a weakening of the U.S. firms' competitiveness. The extent to which other Japanese consumer electronics firms will initiate production in the United States also will be determined in great part by the factors cited previously.

Selection of U.S. Production Sites

Several factors, which have varied among firms, have influenced Japanese color television manufacturers in their selection of U.S. onshore production sites. The different combinations of these weighted factors have dictated where each Japanese manufacturer chose to site its onshore facilities.

Labor Considerations

Access to a relatively inexpensive, disciplined labor-management pool has been a major consideration for several Japanese color television manufacturers in choosing an onshore site. An ample supply of local labor in southern California and proximity to the Mexican border (and thus emigrant labor) strongly influenced Sony's, Mitsubishi's, and Hitachi's decision to locate in this area. Similarly Toshiba's and Sharp's choice of Tennessee and Sanyo's choice of Arkansas reflect a desire to avoid the higher labor costs in more-industrialized areas of the United States. A further attraction of siting in states such as Tennessee and Arkansas has been the promise of high productivity from the local labor and management pools. The Japanese firms have anticipated this high productivity due to the skills, discipline and work ethic found in the local workers, factors that affect the ability to maintain high levels of quality control. Another major attraction of a site such as Toshiba's in Tennessee has been the ability to hire nonunion labor, which represents lower wage scales, less likelihood of disruptive strikes, and the greater possibility of replicating the Japanese work environment.

Transportation Economics

Considerations of transportation costs in terms of both parts supply and market demand have also been important influences on production facility choices. Sony's choice to locate in California was based in part on the fact that it would minimize transportation costs for the higher-technology component supplies shipped from Japan. The existence of a well-established parts manufacturing infrastructure around the Chicago area, which supplied such local firms as Zenith, influenced Matsushita's decision to move there. The presence of extensive railway lines in Memphis and Nashville, Tennessee, was important to Sharp's and Toshiba's respective choices to locate near those urban centers. The same can be said for Sanyo's move to Forrest City, Arkansas, near Memphis, Tennessee, and Matsushita's attraction to the Chicago area. The strong railway services in these areas means reasonable transport costs both for incoming parts supplies and outgoing finished goods. The well-developed transportation system in California, a major market, similarly influenced Sony, Mitsubishi and Hitachi.

Local Incentives

Incentives to invest offered by state and municipal authorities have been important to Japanese color television producers. These incentives have been in the form of various tax breaks or reductions in real estate prices.

Availability of Existing Facilities

In Sanyo's decision to purchase jointly with Sears the existing color television production facilities of the U.S. firm Warwick in Forrest City, Arkansas, and Matsushita's decision to purchase Motorola's operations around Chicago, the question of site selection was already answered in great part by the availability of these plants for purchase. Yet the respective decisions to purchase these preexisting facilities was reinforced, to a greater or lesser degree, by the other factors.

Relevance to Global Business Strategies

The movement by seven Japanese color television manufacturers to U.S. onshore production is but one, albeit crucial, facet of these firms' overall global strategy. Whether through export marketing or, increasingly, through the establishment of regional production and assembly operations, these firms are aggressively endeavoring to extend their global reach. The central element of this strategy is volume production to reduce costs of manufacture. Because the U.S. market is the largest in the world for consumer electronics, it is a critical outlet for the desired high volumes of production that Japanese firms strive for. As the U.S. market has become increasingly closed to direct export, onshore assembly and production has grown in attraction, with onshore facilities serving as outlets for the high production volumes of higher-technology componentry produced in Japan. The policy of moving toward higher volumes of production replicates itself in the Japanese firms' onshore facilities as these facilities continue to increase their output levels or anticipate such an increase. (See table 5-3 for projected increases announced by Japanese onshore manufacturers.)

Table 5-3
Announced Production Increases for Japanese U.S.-Based Plants

Firm	1979 Production Capacity Range	Announced New Production Level	Anticipated Date of New Production Level
Hitachi	36,000– 50,000	180,000	By 1981
Matsushita	700,000-800,000	1,000,000	1980
Mitsubishi	150,000-180,000	187,000	by 1981
Sanyo	700,000-900,000	a	a
Sharp	100,000-120,000	240,000	1980
Sony	500,000-700,000	800,000	1980
Toshiba	300,000-400,000	500,000	By mid-1980

Source: DEWIT, Inc., compilation.

[a]No information available.

In their drive to establish significant economies of scale in color television production, Japanese consumer electronics firms distinguish between those production functions that are best left in Japan and those that may be advantageously located abroad. In effect, Japanese consumer electronics firms are adopting a strategy of the distribution of the production function on a global basis. Japan's color television makers thus are increasing the efficiency of production and supply through the international division of labor.

Although the production of higher-technology componentry and new products is retained, by and large, in Japan, Japanese consumer electronics firms have been relocating to areas where one or more of the following may occur: the cost of manufacture is less than in Japan; local production and distribution operations permit more-effective local marketing; protectionism forces an offshore move (as in the United States and Europe); and a particular offshore assembly or manufacturing site is advantageous to serve a regional (more than one country) market. These considerations require a global approach to international production and marketing and the reconciling of often-conflicting objectives or considerations.

The globalization of the Japanese color televison manufacturers' operations is similar to the current internationalization of the production function occurring in the world automotive industry. In both cases, the standardization of componentry produced and assembled on a worldwide basis in consideration of local cost factors is critical. Standardization of components and the maintenance of Japanese standards of quality control are necessary conditions of such arrangements. Yet the most important feature of componentry standardization in, for example, a range of color television receivers is that significant economies of scale can be achieved for specific componentry.

In following a strategy of distributing the production function on a global basis, Japanese color television manufacturers have been concerned with retaining the production of higher-technology componentry and products at home, at least until the component or product in question has matured, its technology has reached a state of worldwide diffusion, or cost considerations dictate otherwise. This policy serves to preserve Japanese international competiveness in terms of production costs (high-volume production of higher-technology componentry with latest-generation automation) and technological leadership (safeguarding of manufacturing expertise from competitors and stimulation of dynamic growth through concentration of work on front-end technology in parent firms).

Many examples can be cited concerning Japanese onshore facilities' being supplied with higher-technology components from Japanese parent plants. For example, Toshiba's plant in Tennessee plans to increase local procurement to 70 percent but import large-scale integrated circuits (LSIs), integrated circuits (ICs), and ancillary parts from Toshiba in Japan. Additionally, all new printed circuit boards for U.S. assembly are being supplied from Japan; these boards are equipped with new LSI devices and assembled by newly designed automatic robots.

In line with the strategy of keeping the production of advanced componentry and new products at home, the movement onshore by Japanese color television firms permits these firms to switch former domestic color television plants to the manufacturing of more technically advanced and higher value products such as VTRs, video disc units, or technically advanced office equipment. The freeing of domestic color television plants for production of such advanced new products as VTRs through movement of color television manufacture to the United States is resulting in meteoric increases in the annual production volume of these newer products. Domestic Japanese production of VTRs has increased fivefold in the 1976–1978 period, from 286,226 units produced in 1976 to 1,470,859 units in 1978. Such an increase could not have occurred through erection of new production facilities; conversion of existing color television plants was required.

Yet at an early stage in the product life cycle, advanced video equipment also may be manufactured in the United States, and mirroring color television onshore operations the higher-technology componentry for these advanced video products will come from Japan. Mitsubishi was strongly considering the production of video projectors in the United States in 1979, with a key component, the projection tube, to be supplied from Japan.

For Japanese color television manufacturers, a central pillar of their international competitiveness is their advanced manufacturing technology. Typically these Japanese firms are retaining the more technologically advanced manufacturing processes (involving LSI and microprocessor componentry and utilizing high levels of automation) at home. High labor costs in the United States make uncompetitive the labor-intensive assembly work Japanese plants in the United States primarily perform. Therefore Japanese firms are considering increased automated production in the United States, but with technique less advanced and extensive than those used in Japan.

Japanese firms also have several reservations about expanding U.S. procurement. One is the general difficulty they claim they have with U.S. firms (relative to Japanese firms) in achieving and maintaining quality standards, in getting them to adjust parts designs to their specifications, and in covering start-up costs for new procurement. For example, the Sony plant in San Diego finally got a toilet seat manufacturer to fabricate the television console cabinets they needed after screening over twenty local companies unsuccessfully. In the IC field, Japanese firms say they get better slicing (uniformity and flatness) and polishing of silicon wafers from Japanese sources and even in simple items like aluminum capacitors, they have tried but failed to get the cost and quality in the United States that they can get in Japan. In memory devices, Japanese sources are superior in manufacturing metal-oxide semiconductors. U.S. firms are better on high-speed, bipolar ICs, designed in large part from work and capital funding under military-space programs. U.S. firms are also acknowledged as being superior in the design of ICs and software, again as a result of military procurement and capital funding (NASA financed the construction of an entire factory for Fairchild Camera). The design and manufacture of photo masks used in the manufacture of LSIs is another area where U.S. firms are still ahead.

When queried on the type of components and parts for which they might expand procurement from the United States, Japanese firms indicate items or materials that are energy intensive. One item cited is yoke cores for television tubes, for which 20 percent of the cost is energy. With energy costs in Japan running three times that of the United States, this would mean a 40 percent savings on manufacturing such parts in the United States. Another item cited, and for which several companies have invested in new plants (industrial sites in the United States are a fraction of what they cost in Japan), are recording tapes, epoxy materials (made from petrochemicals), and certain silicon materials (ingots).

Another aspect of U.S. production that fits into the Japanese color television firms' overall strategy reflects these firms' commitment to establish and maintain the broadest possible product spread in a given market. U.S. production facilities thus serve as beachheads from which to expand consumer electronics product lines for the U.S. market while avoiding protectionist backlash and being able to gauge and react quickly to U.S. market demand. Sony and Matsushita, for example, have been in the forefront of Japanese manufacturers in the United States in broadening their production of larger-sized screens. Japanese firms are also using their U.S. facilities to produce color televisions with new features. At its Tennessee plant, Toshiba is producing a nineteen-inch color television set with a remote control and digital clock device that memorizes the channels and times of up to six programs a day and automatically follows preprogrammed instructions. Additionally several Japanese U.S. color television plants also produce microwave ovens.

The Japanese firms' ability to move quickly and efficiently into a broader horizontal spread of consumer electronics manufacturing in the United States is reinforced by their already existing broad horizontal production spread in Japan. Final assembly and lower technology production operations in the United States in a wide range of color television models or other consumer electronics products are reinforced by the operations of parent plants in Japan. This is a reflection of the Japanese firms' strategy for global reach of a broad and deep nature. Japanese color television plants in the United States may be supplied with componentry produced in-house, from the parent firms in Japan, or from subsidiaries in areas with inexpensive labor such as Southeast Asia or Mexico. Matsushita, for example, is beginning to supply its Franklin Park, Illinois, plant with color television chassis and tuner assemblies from its new Mexican plant in Tijuana, and using printed circuit boards from Japan.

Finally, in regard to their global corporate strategies, Japanese firms may use their U.S.-based production facilities as the hub of a hemispheric marketing operation. There are indications that a percentage of color televisions and other consumer electronic products assembled in U.S. facilities are, to some degree, being exported to Canadian and South and Central America markets. Japanese facilities in the United States thus are taking on the characteristic of regional production centers, at least until local plants are established in Central or South America.

Profitability

Although information on the profitability of Japanese color television manufacturers' U.S. operations is not readily available, that which is available suggests that these onshore facilities currently are not operating on a profitable basis. For Japanese firms that established U.S. plants in 1978 or later (Mitsubishi, Toshiba, Sharp, and Hitachi), it is still too soon to determine profitability. Yet for Japanese firms that established facilities prior to 1978 (Sony, Sanyo, and Matsushita), most signs point to operating losses.

After acquiring the former money-losing Warwick television manufacturing operation in Forrest City, Arkansas, Sanyo began turning a profit in a short time. Sanyo Manufacturing Company, Sanyo's U.S. subsidiary, announced a profit of $1.8 million for the fiscal year ending November 30, 1977, but Sanyo had slipped into the red by the end of 1978 and has been there since. In the third quarter ending August 31, 1979, it reported a loss of $580,000, raising its total deficit for the nine-month period to $1.29 million. Although the company had a modest sales improvement in the last quarter of 1979, it suffered from a strike that shut down the factory from August 5 to October 1. The strike and the start-up of deflection yoke production during this quarter further depressed financial results.

For Sony's U.S. operations, there are indications that it has been meeting with profitability difficulties due primarily to severe price and product competition in the U.S. market. In Matsushita's case, profits have also not been readily forthcoming. Matsushita purchased Motorola's three U.S. television plants for $108 million. By consolidating the production of color television into one plant and embarking on a two-year, multimillion dollar modernization and automation program, Matsushita hoped to make its U.S. operation profitable within three years. In those three years, Quasar reportedly encountered large losses, but in the last two quarters of 1977 it turned a profit. Nevertheless on an annual basis Matsushita apparently has never had a profitable year in its U.S. operation.

Magnavox, the American subsidiary of the Dutch firm N.V. Philips, has not faired much better than its Japanese counterparts. In 1975 Magnavox posted an operating loss of $3.1 million, although the operating income was $19.3 million and $7.2 million in 1976 and 1977, respectively. In 1978 an operating loss of $2.1 million was again recorded. North American Philips Corporation, Magnavox's parent company, in its annual report attributed the loss to severe price competition in major product areas, a market shift to lower unit costs, and increased operating costs.

The currently unfavorable profit picture for the U.S. facilities of Japanese color television manufacturers should not be taken as an indication of their future financial health. Several factors should be considered in predicting these operations' future profitability. Foremost among these is the Japanese firms' corporate policy of taking a longer-term view of their operations. Although U.S. firms tend to be more concerned with current profitability, Japanese firms are more inclined to suffer current operating setbacks in anticipation of future earnings. Japanese color television plants thus are encountering a period of growing pains, which it is hoped will subside as the following dimensions are more effectively brought into play.

Volume Production

Japanese onshore plants have been increasing their production capacity or anticipate such increases. By moving along the learning curve and achieving greater economies of scale, the Japanese firms hope to reduce operating costs. Optimal plant sizes for various television manufacturing operations are commonly estimated as follows: stamping and cabinetmaking, 50,000 units; picture tube manufacturing, 300,000 units; and printed circuits, over 500,000 units.

Broadening of Product Range

American demand for the high mark-up, larger-screen color televisions, which are the real money earners, is at present largely met by the U.S. color television makers. Yet Japanese firms are beginning to challenge the U.S. firms in this product range. Sanyo, for example, has become the third largest U.S. producer of large-screen color televisions (nineteen-inch and over). Sony is also intent on increasing its output of larger-screen color televisions.

Narrowing of Production Costs

Although a specific breakdown of respective costs of production for U.S.-sited and offshore-sited plants of U.S. and Japanese color television manufacturers is not possible with available information, a general comparative picture of these costs can be drawn. In the United States, the respective costs for U.S.-owned and Japanese-owned plants would seem to favor the U.S. firms, due primarily to respective costs for componentry. But the Japanese firms stand a good chance of reducing their costs below those of U.S. firms in time. In regard to U.S.-owned and Japanese-owned plants on offshore sites, the Japanese firms most likely enjoy a cost advantage due to more-efficient manufacturing procedures.

By way of assessing the respective costs of manufacture for U.S.-owned and Japanese-owned production facilities in the U.S., a comparative analysis of several key factors is useful.

Labor Costs: Because the U.S.-and Japanese-owned firms perform similar operations in the United States and there is, on average, no significant difference in site location in terms of labor costs, these costs should be roughly equivalent between U.S.-owned and Japanese-owned plants. The somewhat greater success of Japanese firms in obtaining nonunionized labor could be an advantage to them.

Manufacturing Costs: Although it is difficult to gauge these respective costs, the advantage would seem to be with the Japanese plants. The Japanese firms are showing an increasing inclination to automate, with little similar inclination apparent on the part of U.S. firms. U.S. firms' disinclination to automate, relative to Japanese firms, is based primarily on three factors: relative inaccessibility of capital for automation investment; a reward and penalty structure in U.S. firms that discourages engineers from movement toward fuller automation; and union pressure to minimize job reductions.

The stronger Japanese propensity to make the necessary capital expenditures for automation can result in reduced labor costs, higher production volumes, and greater quality assurance, all contributing to a cost advantage. Matsushita, for example, spent heavily on automation in its Illinois plant, with the consequence that it spent only $4 million to pay warranty claims on its Quasar sets made there, while two years earlier its previous owner had spent $22 million.

The ability of the Japanese firms to maintain the high levels of quality control prevalent in Japanese-sited plants may also translate into cost reductions. When Sanyo took over the Warwick facility in Arkansas, it was able to cut the postretail failure rate of television sets produced at that plant from 10 percent of factory shipments to less than 2 percent. Similarly the

Japanese onshore manufacturers appear to be much more concerned with the quality of components they procure in the United States than are their American competitors. Whereas most U.S. color television manufacturers provide only general guidelines and specifications for required components and parts, Japanese firms such as Sony issue their suppliers product manuals with detailed specifications. Although the primary goal of such practices is to maintain component quality standards, an advantageous side-effect for Japanese firms with strong quality-control practices may be a cost reduction through reduction of defects and warranty claims.

Additionally the degree to which Japanese firms can replicate their domestic production processes in their U.S. plants may affect relative costs favorably. In taking over existing U.S. factories, the Japanese have simultaneously improved both quality and productivity. Although these improvements have not resulted in immediate profits, they should contribute to profitability in the longer run.

Component Procurement: The U.S. color television manufacturers procure their componentry from offshore sites with inexpensive labor to a much greater degree than do Japanese color television plants in the United States. U.S. and Japanese onshore plants obtain their componentry from one of three sources, with the first source being most typical: subsidiary firms, special arrangements with U.S. or Japanese firms, or independent component firms in such lower-wage countries as Taiwan, Korea, or Mexico. Of the four major U.S. firms, GTE, RCA, and Zenith all obtain the bulk of their printed circuit board assemblies from either Taiwan or Mexico; among the U.S.-sited plants of Matsushita, Mitsubishi, Sanyo, Sony, and Toshiba, only Mitsubishi brings in printed circuit board assemblies from Southeast Asia, with the other firms obtaining this component from the more labor-expensive United States or Japan.

For chassis subassembly work, all four major U.S. firms rely on feeder plants in Mexico or Taiwan; RCA has a chassis subassembly plant in both countries. Among the Japanese firms, only Matsushita uses chassis subassemblies from an offshore site with inexpensive labor, Mexico. The other Japanese firms procure these subassemblies in either the United States or Japan.

For active electronic components, such as transistors or integrated circuits, while all the four major U.S. firms procure from both the United States and Japan, they also obtain these components in either Mexico or Taiwan.

By comparison, while Matsushita and Sanyo procure some of these components from plants in Taiwan, Mitsubishi, Sony, and Toshiba rely exclusively on higher-priced sources in the United States or Japan. Magnavox procures all of its active electronic components, printed circuit board assemblies, and chassis subassemblies in either the United States or Japan. At present it appears that the U.S. firms benefit from a cost advantage in terms of componentry sourcing. The *Japan Economic Journal* states the case in stronger terms:

> Because of the present production arrangements, color TVs manufactured in the U.S. by Japanese producers are not particularly competitive with those made by RCA, Zenith, General Electric Co. and other American manufacturers who produce chassis in Taiwan, Mexico or Singapore.[2]

As a result, Hitachi, a relative newcomer to production in the United States, is looking to its Taiwan subsidiary as a supplier of chassis and major subassemblies to feed its Compton, California, plant.

Japanese firms producing in the United States have not been procuring from existing componentry plants in Southeast Asia in part because of U.S. import restrictions on subassemblies from these countries but also because several of the Japanese firms have indicated publicly that they intend to establish more vertically integrated color television facilities in the United States. Japanese firms are indicating a desire to increase local U.S. content (in part, it would seem, for political and public-relations reasons); to the extent to which this occurs, this may translate into cost saving (for example, through reduced transportation costs) but this is far from certain.

Additionally Japanese firms are moving to obtain selected componentry from offshore sites with inexpensive labor, such as Mexico and Singapore. Matsushita's decision to establish a componentry feeder plant in Mexico for its U.S. plant was designed to reduce Quasar's operating costs. The extent to which Japanese firms can procure componentry offshore, where manufacturing costs are lower, will result in better profits. It is too early to tell whether these moves will translate into componentry cost savings for the Japanese manufacturers.

Overall the Japanese color television firms with U.S. plants have the capabilities and resources to produce at the same cost as U.S. firms in America, if not at lower costs. Yet the current generally unprofitable nature of the Japanese firms' U.S. operations indicates that these firms are not yet able to take full advantage of their inherent strengths in terms of process technology, management, and propensity for capital expenditures for production upgrading.

Notes

1. See Hiroki Tsurumi and Yoshi Tsurumi, "A Bayesian Test of the Product Life Cycle as Applied to the U.S. Demand for Color TV Sets," *International Economic Review* 21, no. 3 (October 1980):583-597.

2. *Japan Economic Journal* (August 14, 1979), p. 14.

U.S. Business Response to Japanese Competition

Comparative Performance of U.S. Manufacturers

During the course of the 1970s the health of U.S. firms in the U.S. consumer electronics industry worsened appreciably. Increasing competition from foreign, primarily Japanese, firms explains much of the decline of the U.S. industry but does not tell the whole story. Poor management, particularly in terms of focusing corporate strategy on short-term tactics, has also played a significant role in this decline. There were eighteen U.S. manufacturers of television receivers operating in the United States in 1968; by 1980 there were only four U.S. firms. The overall profit and employment figures do not paint a much better picture.

The American firms in the industry have been operating at declining levels of profit. The ratio of net operating profit before taxes to net sales of the U.S. color television manufacturers on their overall television operations declined from 8.7 percent in 1971 to 5.8 percent in 1973; in 1974, an operating loss of 1.2 percent was recorded. The industry virtually broke even in 1975 with an operating profit of 0.6 percent, followed by a profit ratio of 3.7 percent in 1976. This improvement was largely attributable to the overall operating profits of two large domestic producers, GE and RCA, both of them diversified-product companies. By 1978, though, the industry profit ratio had again declined, to 1.5 percent. Profitability rates for all U.S. manufacturing, in contrast, were approximately 8.8 percent in 1978.

The U.S. television industry has also suffered substantial unemployment and underemployment over the past decade. The average number of total persons employed in U.S. television receiver assembly plants declined each year during the 1971-1975 period, from a high of 42,920 in 1971 to a low of 28,446 in 1975, before slightly increasing to 28,851 in the first nine months of 1976. By 1979 the total number of workers employed in the industry had dropped to 26,190, a decrease of 38 percent from the 1971 level. A simlar trend obtained in employment levels of production and related workers—declining from 36,694 in 1971 to 22,470 in 1979, or by 38 percent again.

There are significant differences among U.S. firms in the industry in terms of their level of output and sources of earnings, dependence upon television manufacture as a percentage of total output, and the profitability

97

of television compared to other product lines. These characteristics have conditioned response patterns to competition in the color television and VTR fields, which in turn have important implications for U.S. employment, income, foreign-exchange balances, and investments in U.S. plant and R&D.

At one extreme, Zenith almost exclusively manufactures consumer electronics products, primarily color television receivers; in the *Fortune* list of the five hundred largest U.S. industrial corporations, Zenith ranked 270 in 1979, as compared to 259 in 1978. At the other extreme, General Electric was ranked by *Fortune* as the ninth largest industrial corporation in the United States in 1979, and consumer electronics sales composed less than a quarter of all its business.

The major U.S. firms in the industry have shown signs of declining or stagnant corporate health in the past few years. Using as a measure annual net income as a percentage of annual sales, GE and GTE maintained a level of 6 percent in 1978 and 1979, while RCA dropped from 4 percent in 1978 to 3 percent in 1979. Zenith, which is the best indicator for the consumer electronics industry given its heavy involvement, saw its net income as a percentage of sales drop from 2 percent in 1978 to 1 percent in 1979.

An indicator of the priority individual companies assign to new-product development in general is annual R&D expenditures. Breakdowns of these figures into product groups are not available, and therefore they give no indication of how much is spent on television-related R&D. In the United States, color television manufacturers' investments in R&D averaged 2.3 percent of annual sales in 1978. The Japanese consumer electronics industry, by comparison, had an average R&D expenditure level of 3.5 percent of annual sales in 1978. Zenith's and GE's R&D expenditures as a percentage of annual sales in 1978 were 3 and 2.7 percent, respectively, and GTE's and RCA's expenditures were lower, at 1.5 and 2.1 percent, respectively. Compared with the more-dynamic and faster-growing U.S. computer industry, which averages 9 percent of sales on R&D expenditures, these figures are dismally low. The averages of these figures are even below the total U.S. business R&D spending average, which was 2.4 percent of GNP in the mid-1970s, having dropped from 2.9 percent in the late 1960s.

When R&D sponsored by the U.S. government or other customers is included, these figures are significantly increased. (Zenith is the only one of the four U.S. firms that conducts R&D solely on internally generated funds.) Both RCA and GE receive over 60 percent of their R&D funds from customer or government contracts, while GTE's customer and government funding is only a quarter of the total expended.

Response Patterns of U.S. Firms

A variety of response patterns emerges in examining the way in which U.S. television manufacturers have dealt with adversity in recent years, beginning with the first wave of import competition in 1970, rising U.S. labor costs, sluggish market demand resulting from the 1974 recession, and finally the surge in Japanese imports since 1975. Certain firms instigated legal action in an effort to redress grievances they attributed to imports; others undertook radical changes in the corporate entity such as divestiture of unprofitable product lines or the acquisition of rapid-growth operations; and some made positive efforts to improve products or to reduce production costs (significantly, though, not through automation in most cases but rather by moving offshore with existing technology). The particular response or combination of repsonses is in large part a function of the extent to which a particular company is highly diversified and thereby has a diversity of options from which to select. A related factor is the extent to which a company is committed to maintaining itself as a leader in color television manufacture or is satisfied simply to maintain a presence in the market. Some response patterns have served to reinforce the competitiveness of the U.S. industry, while others clearly work toward its demise.

Legal Actions

Over the past several years, the U.S. industry has made numerous allegations that Japanese television manufacturers have achieved their substantial share of the U.S. market through the use of unfair trade practices. Legal and financial redress has been sought through a variety of import-relief petitions and litigation designed to impose U.S. import restrictions on the Japanese firms. This pattern of response to Japanese competition has met with uneven success, as in the case of the import relief petition brought by COMPACT. Early in 1980, however, the U.S. Treasury Department, after a lengthy investigation, imposed a $46 million dumping penalty on imports of Japanese color and black-and-white sets shipped to the United States in 1972 and the first half of 1973.

A suit charging unfair import competition was brought to court by GTE Sylvania in 1976. Rather than contest the charges in expensive and lengthy litigation, the five accused Japanese companies replied to the complaint by signing consent orders, which prohibit, without admitting guilt, price fixing, marketing in a predatory manner, and illegal blockage of sales by U.S. companies in Japan.

Zenith Radio Corporation has been the most determined and persistent of the U.S. companies seeking legal redress for alleged grievances or violations by the Japanese companies. Its most publicized effort involved a countervailing duty case against Japanese color television importers, charging that Japan's alleged practice of remitting the commodity taxes imposed on manufacturers once the products are exported constituted a bounty or grant within the meaning of the U.S. countervailing duty statute. The U.S. Supreme Court considered the case in June 1979 and rejected Zenith's arguments. Zenith also pressed its case against Japanese television manufacturers in the antitrust area, charging that the firms, in collaboration with U.S. private-brand retailers, have conspired to monopolize the U.S. market.

Individually as well as collectively, these accusations against the Japanese raise some important and difficult questions for the U.S. economy. One is, how effective are safeguards and other import-relief measures against the consequences arising from differences in economic systems? It is generally agreed that the uniquely cooperative relationship among the business, banking, and government communities in Japan, in addition to the country's policies for encouraging collaborative arrangements in marketing, production, and R&D among companies, give Japanese industry a decided advantage over American firms. These advantages are further reinforced by tax and credit measures aimed at reinforcing business innovators and risk takers.

A related question concerns the extent to which the U.S. government should and can go in enforcing domestic legislation outside its borders. This issue bears particular relevance to the complaint brought by GTE Sylvania and the Zenith antitrust suit. In both cases, judgments were being requested based upon the very structure and competitive behavior of a Japanese industry. Finally, Zenith's case before the U.S. Supreme Court forced the issue of whether the U.S. government should retaliate against the widespread practice by major trading partners of rebating indirect taxes to manufacturers on exported goods as part of an overall export promotion strategy. Had the decision been favorable to Zenith, it would have set a precedent on which other U.S. industries could seek the imposition of countervailing duties on other products.

Offshore Movements

Every U.S.-owned television manufacturer today operates offshore manufacturing facilities. The percentage of such manufacturing is on average 50 percent of total value added for RCA, General Electric, GTE Sylvania, and now Zenith.[1] This phenomenon dates back to 1960 when

U.S. component companies established overseas plants so they could compete with importer pricing. Among the first that did so were audio manufacturers that integrated imported electronics and record changers into stereo compacts and consoles. Coming later were black-and-white television makers that set up shop in Taiwan and Mexico. In the audio equipment field today, virtually every U.S. marketer has offshore relationships for either its manufacturing or procurement operation. The major companies operate assembly facilities in the United States, and many manufacture speakers or cabinets in the United States or buy them from other U.S. companies.

With the pattern already well established, it is not unusual that U.S. color television manufacturers have followed suit. The late 1960s and early 1970s witnessed the first offshore movement of American television manufacturers, but the bulk of this production was in low-technology, labor-intensive assembly operations. Additional incentives to move offshore came from sections 806 and 807 of the U.S. Tariff Code, permitting the reexport of goods in these categories to the U.S. market taxed only on the value added from abroad. The Overseas Private Investment Corporation (OPIC), which at the time was relatively free from the constraints under which it currently operates, may also have contributed to this offshore movement by insuring U.S. investments in low-wage economies for reexport of goods back to the United States for final assembly.

Increased competition from Japan coupled with the recession in 1974 gave further impetus to offshore manufacture. At that time, U.S. firms were finding that their production technologies were no longer competitive in a high-wage economy, and rather than investing in upgraded and modernized production techniques and redesigning the set, most chose to move a substantial portion of their operations offshore. The result of this second exodus from U.S. production was to lock U.S. companies into the existing state-of-the-art technology and to eliminate to a large degree any further need to retool and automate. This particular response pattern has placed an expanded burden on U.S. labor market adjustments in terms of job skills, plant locations, and experience-wage structures. Yet, it is difficult to ascertain exactly when and to what extent U.S. television manufacturers have moved production offshore because it is usually done quietly and in small, discrete segments, affecting one or two individual communities in the United States at any one time.

Most of General Electric's circuit boards and other color components are made in Singapore. Magnavox imports from the Taiwanese plant of its Dutch parent firm Philips. RCA manufactures and assembles components in Taiwan and began moving color chassis operations to Mexico in 1975. GTE Sylvania purchased a plant in Taiwan in 1975 for production of televisions (both black-and-white and color) and has operated a color chassis and parts facility in Mexico since 1973. And Zenith, even before its September 1977 decision to increase substantially offshore production, made black-and-white television sets and some color circuit boards in Taiwan and picture-tube guns and deflection yoke parts in Mexico.

Zenith's offshore movement in the fall of 1977—entailing the release of 5,600 workers and shifting their jobs to the company's Mexico and Taiwan facilities—came after three years of declining sales and profits. The announcement of a decision by an American electronics or television manufacturer to move offshore had long lost any element of surprise, but the announcement by Zenith sent powerful shock waves throughout the industry, as well as those groups concerned with the industry. The reason was that Zenith had long resisted the temptation to move a major part of its manufacturing operation abroad, advertising "premium-quality products made in the U.S." and claiming that talk of declining U.S. craftsmanship and productivity was "bunk." In any event, the action signaled that the U.S. company most committed to retaining its U.S. labor force had to reduce significantly its U.S.-manufactured content.

Associations with Foreign Firms

Another pattern of response taken by American corporations to their recent problems has been to associate with a Japanese company for the purpose of marketing or joint production. This has been most evident in the case of VTRs. That the Japanese were the exclusive developer of a home VTR that is both affordable and sufficiently feature laden to attract American consumers put U.S. firms in the industry in a rather awkward predicament: they could accelerate R&D efforts on their own VTR models and hope to develop a commercial product before the Japanese captured too large a share of the U.S. market, or they could market the Japanese-made VTR until such time as they could manufacture and incorporate their own proprietary electronics into an American-designed model.

Most of the U.S. firms in the industry have decided that opportunities today are too great to stay out of the market and have purchased the equipment in Japan, put on their own logo and trade names, and run them through their own quality-control procedures and into distribution channels. Thus far RCA, Magnavox, Sylvania, and GE, along with the Japanese firms Mitsubishi and JVC, are committed to selling Matsushita-designed machines, while Zenith, Sears, Sanyo, Toshiba, and Sony will be selling Sony's Betamax.

A relatively low profit margin on VTR units has compelled U.S. firms to market the new products aggressively, but the marketers believe that as sales go up over the next few years, profit margins will be enlarged. A more compelling reason for U.S. firms to market Japanese-made VTRs has been the low entry costs into this new market (as compared to tooling up for manufacture), combined with the expectation that having a VTR to market will enhance television sales and reinforce the rest of their product line through trade-name association. Once sales increase substantially, the marketing costs can be spread over more units, and profit margins should improve.

Most of the marketing agreements contain a clause permitting the company to manufacture the VTR under license in its own facilities, but none of the American firms as yet has taken up this option. The high-precision components and parts for VTR equipment appear to be too costly to manufacture in the United States and logistically difficult to produce and procure offshore. This particular response pattern underlines the U.S. corporate proclivity to take the most expedient way to earn income. The pressure to develop a commercially viable and alternative home product has been lifted through the marketing arrangements, and in the meantime the Japanese are enhancing their own design engineering capabilities and seizing the opportunity to move quickly down the learning curve in VTR manufacture.

The alternative product upon which American firms, most notably RCA (and Magnavox), have concentrated R&D efforts has been the video disc system, which promises to retail in a much lower price range than the VTR. Simpler in design and technology and cheaper in materials, the video disc only plays prerecorded programs (captured on a record) and cannot be used to record on-air television or homemade programs. RCA, which has been working on the video disc since the late 1960s, is the U.S. company closest to bringing a product to market. Major obstacles have been in the areas of price and the availability of software for the system. It is RCA's contention that a competitive disc system must retail at around $400, a level not yet realized by the company. In addition, RCA is not yet confident that the supply of available records on the market today is sufficiently large or diverse to encourage consumers to purchase the video disc player.

In a more comprehensive attempt to associate with a Japanese firm, the first joint venture for television manufacture was negotiated between GE and Hitachi in 1978 but was never realized due to lack of necessary approval from the Antitrust Division of the Justice Department. GE, with its generations of experience in television and related electronics manufacture, was to contribute the facilities and personnel to the equally owned venture, while Hitachi was to provide technology and some money. GE hoped to boost its U.S. market share, which had rested at around 6 percent for several years previously, and also anticipated receiving from Hitachi new and advanced product and process technology. Hitachi, on the other hand, which had only marginal success in penetrating the U.S. market and that largely through the private brand retailers, expected to take advantage of GE's trade name and well-developed national distribution and servicing network.

Some industry observers have disapproved of GE's response to adversity, labeling the attempted joint venture as an admission of defeat. To the contrary, its action would have contributed more to reinforcing U.S. jobs and production than would offshore production or leaving the business altogether. There is good reason to believe that because this opportunity was not made available to GE, the company eventually will phase out of television production, devoting its resources to higher-yielding, faster-growth products.

Diversification

In an effort to reinforce and diversify corporate earnings that have eroded in the face of Japanese competition and rising costs, some corporate managements of U.S. television manufacturers have sought to acquire operations in totally unrelated product lines. This development is by no means unique to the television industry. Over the past decade, U.S. management generally has shown an increased tendency to shift from one industry to another, seeking a higher return on stockholder's investments. What is significant and at the same time disturbing about several of these movements is that they sometimes take the company away from technology-intensive activity and into low-technology service work. At least this has been the trend in the diversification programs of U.S. color television firms.

RCA is the most notable example in the industry of a firm's diversifying into the service sector; over the past several years it has acquired Random House Publishing Company, Hertz Rent-a-Car, Oriel Foods in the United Kingdom, Coronet Carpet, and Banquet Frozen Foods. These acquisitions were part of RCA's strategy to move into operations that promised to provide steady earnings and that were as sensitive to the overall performance of the economy as had been its traditional electronics operations. More recently, RCA has restated its commitment to remain a high-technology company and has sold off its Random House, Oriel Foods, and Banquet Frozen Foods operations (while purchasing a cash-earning credit company). In a similar move into higher-yielding activity, GE further diversified its already broad base of operations in 1976 by acquiring Utah International, the Australian-based mining concern. By 1977 Utah's operations represented 5 percent of GE's sales and contributed 18 percent to overall corporate profits.

GTE Sylvania has made two acquisitions in recent years in an effort to fortify its home entertainment line against further incursions by the Japanese. The first was the purchase of Ford Philco's television line in

1974, in the belief that Sylvania's and Philco's combined market share would lead to higher volume production, reduced costs per set, and improved profits. This expectation has not yet materialized. Sylvania's second acquisition was in a related product line but in the service sector. For some time, the company had run a television sales and leasing operation for hospitals. To augment and complement the operation, it purchased certain assets of the Institutional Electronics Unit of Motorola in 1976, which leased sets to the hotel and motel market.

The regrettable aspect to much of the recent diversification pattern as a response to Japanese competition is that it diverts management talents and growth resources (R&D efforts and capital investments) to lower-technology industries that promise quick returns and contribute to the further decline of the troubled product. While the higher-yielding service industries may draw upon managerial and marketing expertise, they tend to place few demands on design-engineering capabilities. If profits from the service-oriented concerns were channeled into new-product generation or into redesign of products or production systems, one could take some consolation in this trend, but there is little evidence that this is the case thus far.

Divestiture

Declining profits and Japanese competition have taken the greatest toll on small U.S. producers of consumer electronic products, most notably producers of television receivers. At best these companies have chosen to divest themselves of lesser product lines, exemplified by Zenith's sale in 1977 of its hearing aid business and in 1978 of its watchmaking division, both of which were losing money. This streamlining of company operations was undertaken in the belief that exclusive attention and commitment of corporate resources to television production would pull the company out of its slump and regain its competitiveness. At worst, these companies have been forced to divest themselves of their television operations, which in most cases meant selling out altogether to a larger corporation.

In recent years, a number of U.S. television manufacturers have met this fate: Admiral was acquired by Rockwell, International, in 1973, which discounted Admiral's television operations in 1978 because they kept losing money; Motorola was acquired by Matsushita in 1974; Magnavox, by North American Philips, the American affiliate of Philips Gloeilampen-fabrieken of the Netherlands in 1974; Ford Motor Company's Philco consumer electronics business, by GTE-Sylvania in that same year; and Warwick was acquired by Sanyo in 1976.

Significantly three of the five buyers have been foreign competitors, serving to enlarge their market share in the United States. To the extent that these acquisitions retain or expand (if only production) jobs in the United States, they are desirable, at least in the short run. In cases where the foreign investment produces a lower percentage U.S.-content set, which displaces a U.S.-manufactured set with a higher percentage of U.S. components, U.S. employment is undermined and the competitiveness of the foreign industry enhanced.

Upgrading of Television Technology

We include the upgrading of technology in this section more as a highly desirable pattern of response from the perspective of U.S. economic interests than as one actually being adopted by U.S. industry. In some cases, U.S. firms have made an effort to upgrade their technology to enhance competitiveness against the Japanese, but frequently the effort has been too little, too late.

The U.S. industry, under pressure to maintain profits in the face of new and rising costs, has taken a harder look at R&D spending and has grown to demand quick and measurable results, thus taking money out of longer-range research. Expenditures are largely limited to maintenance of existing product lines, and less and less is going into new product development. Most R&D efforts focus on what are essentially cosmetic alterations—making sets easier for consumers to use and providing new marketing themes for manufacturers to use in advertising annual model changes. These changes have included remote control, now available on most sets, automatic channel selector (or "varactor" tuner), and automatic picture control, represented by trade names such as Color Trac (RCA) and Color Sentry (Zenith).

All too often, the U.S. industry's earnest R&D efforts are flawed by technical indecision and an aversion to aggressive risk taking. The experience of Motorola in the 1960s illustrates this well. In 1968 Motorola came out with the first all-solid-state color television, representing a major technological breakthrough for the industry. Nearly four years passed before any other manufacturer built a comparable set. This interim period would have given Motorola ample time to capture a large segment of the market with its superior sets, but top management believed that the cost of replacing vacuum tubes with transistors was too great to justify converting any but the top-of-the-line consoles into solid state. Priced at over $600, however, console models had limited appeal. It was not until RCA and Zenith offered complete all-solid-state lines that Motorola even began replacing a substantial number of transistors with tubes in its sets, in model year 1973. By that time, however, the market opportunity was lost. Motorola had a mere 8 percent of the market against Zenith's 22.5 percent and RCA's 20.3 percent. In the following year, Motorola was forced to sell its television plant assets to Matsushita.

Significantly it was the Japanese industry that first appreciated and fully commercialized solid-state technology. The major merits of complete transistorization—energy conservation and a quick turn-on picture—held great appeal to Japanese consumers. Hitachi was the first Japanese firm to incorporate the new technology in its set, in 1969, and thereby increased substantially its own market share in Japan. Nearly all Japanese color receivers were changed to the full transistor type the next year, while the vacuum tube and hybrids of vacuum tubes and transistors continued to be produced in the United States for several years thereafter. This was the turning point in the technological advancement of Japanese over American industry.

Motorola's history contains another example of an American firm's effort to upgrade its technology being too little too late. In 1968, the company launched an aggressive expansion program, adding 50 percent more floor space for manufacturing operations and constructing a new plant in Taiwan. The gains Motorola obtained with this greatly expanded production capacity, however, were eroded by the failure to automate its production processes as quickly as its competitors had. (Until Matsushita's complete retooling and automating of the production facilities of Motorola's Franklin Park, Illinois plant, a substantial portion of the component insertion for color sets was done by hand.)

A recent major Zenith undertaking in R&D, under a joint development program with Corning Glass, is another illustration of a not altogether successful effort to upgrade technology. Faced with the economic recession of 1974-1975 and intense price competition from both Japanese and U.S. firms, Zenith chose to push further automation in existing plants and to funnel research funds into a joint-venture program with Corning Glass to develop a new picture tube designed to lower costs by as much as 20 percent. The new Chromocolor II picture, with a unique extended field lens electron gun, featured a high-resolution picture and a slimmer cabinet. Although the new tube represented a significant innovation, the projected cut in production costs did not materialize, primarily because of problems Corning encountered. Those aspects of the tube developed by Zenith, however, have been retained in the line and, according to Zenith, are becoming the industry standard.

Interestingly RCA faced up to these same pressures in 1974-1975 with a more successful combination of R&D and production relocation. It was at this time that RCA moved some of its assembly operations to its Juarez, Mexico, facility, which serves as a feeder plant to its Bloomington, Indiana, plant, and developed a new, low-cost chassis. Together the two actions cut manufacturing costs considerably, with the new chassis design and not the cost of Mexican labor producing the greatest cost savings, according to RCA. If the claim is true, it is all the more regrettable that RCA did not choose to manufacture the new chassis in its U.S. facilities.

In contrast to these accounts of flawed R&D efforts by U.S. firms, the trade literature abounds with reports of successful campaigns by Japanese firms to reduce parts count, automate production, and improve quality control. The Japanese are aggressively designing and engineering for production in their own high-wage economy, whereas American firms are clearly retrenching in both R&D and U.S.-based production.

Comparison of U.S.-Japanese Response to Consumer Preferences

Looking at the relative performances of U.S. and Japanese consumer electronics firms in the 1970s, one is tempted to conclude that Japanese firms have done a better job of adapting to shifts in consumer preferences. Clearly Japanese firms succeeded in exploiting demand in product segments, such as portable sets, long ignored by the U.S. industry. Yet if they wanted to break into the lucrative U.S. market, Japanese firms had little choice but to start by concentrating on the lower-priced end of the product range. It is thus difficult to discern which consideration Japanese firms were responding to—market penetration or an untapped consumer preference for a smaller, portable set—because they are closely related. Japanese firms were able to dovetail their response to both these considerations. Similarly the Japanese firms have been able to dovetail a response to an increasing consumer preference for quality with production strategies (such as, automation) that enhance quality. Yet one could well argue that these production strategies were the offspring of corporate strategies based on the learning curve and that increased quality was only one of several potential benefits. One could also argue that Japanese firms have stressed quality to dispel consumer fears about products made in Japan.

There remains the question of which came first: the marketing strategy or the consumer demand, the production strategy or the consumer preference? Have the Japanese been lucky in that their corporate strategies have fit well with consumer demands, or have they been altering corporate strategies in accordance to perceived consumer preferences? To their credit, Japanese firms do make special efforts to detect and respond to consumer wishes, prompted by an increasingly discriminating buying public that has developed a strong intolerance toward poor quality. For example, design engineers at Matsushita are required to spend six months selling and servicing products in the company's retail outlets, followed by several months working on the assembly line, experiences that give them a first-hand sense of consumer preferences and of how to design a product for maximum productivity and reliability.

Nonetheless, Japanese firms may simply have been well positioned to take advantage of the shift in demand that occurred in the U.S. market around 1975, without having to make any adjustments. This in no way absolves U.S. firms for failing to adjust. Not only were U.S. producers closer to and presumably more attuned to the domestic market, but even after the market had shifted toward table and portable models, U.S. manufacturers emphasized the production of console models.

U.S. producers were apparently lulled by their continued confidence in the pulling power of brand names, thus believing that consumers would think of brand name before quality in making a purchasing decision. This strategy contains the seeds of its own demise because poor quality eventually will undermine brand-name appeal. Yet U.S. firms did not adjust to the change in consumer demand until they had lost appreciable market shares to Japanese competition.

In contrast to the Japanese, most U.S. firms paid little attention in the past to quality. To their credit, RCA and Zenith eventually became cognizant and adjusted. At Zenith, quality is no longer sacrificed to productivity objectives, representing a significant change in management attitude. Nonetheless price still seems to play a more significant role in the introduction of a new product for U.S. firms than for their Japanese competitors; this has proved to be the case for both VTRs and video discs.

U.S. firms have also continued to rely heavily on advertising to reinforce the brand-name determinant. Thus some U.S. firms have compensated for advertising costs by providing relatively low dealer profit margins; the result is that retailers give stronger support to foreign television brands at the point of sale. A similar situation may be developing with regard to VTR sales. Melco (Mitsubishi) offers dealers profit margins of 30 to 35 percent per unit, while U.S. brands typically provide dealer margins of only 5 to 6 percent.

In sum, it appears that there has been a significant difference between the response patterns of U.S. color television manufacturers and those of their Japanese competitors, both in emphasis on factors determining consumer choice and in the time frame of response. The brand-name determinant is still the most important purchaser consideration for U.S. firms, and they have acted accordingly; their relatively high level of advertising expenditures bear witness to this. Similarly the U.S. firms have been belatedly responsive to marketplace considerations concerning price and quality. Yet unlike the Japanese, the U.S. color television producers' responses to these considerations have not necessarily been prompted by perceived consumer preferences. Japanese firms, on the other hand, seem to be much more aggressive than their U.S. counterparts in responding to consumer preferences. This could well have been a major factor in giving the Japanese firms initial access to and, perhaps, eventual dominance of the American market.

U.S. Government Reaction: Orderly Market Agreements

The OMA represents a delicate compromise between industry and labor interests, which have insisted that higher quotas be imposed on Japanese color television imports, and U.S. trade and foreign policy officials who are loathe to take measures against Japan that are suggestive of either retaliation or protection. The publicly acknowledged purpose of the Orderly Marketing Agreement was to provide U.S. manufacturers a limited period of relief from increasing import competition, sufficient to permit a serious effort at revitalization by the industry. Yet a side letter to the OMA accepted by MITI from the U.S. government committed the Japanese firms to have for individual color television sets a value-added content of not less than 50 percent produced in the United States. As a result, Mitsubishi, Toshiba, Hitachi, and Sharp established manufacturing facilities in the United States within two years of the OMA's signing. In effect, the OMA represented an inconvenience to those Japanese firms that did not have U.S.-based operations and triggered the establishment of such facilities before those firms may have wished. Yet the agreement did little in terms of restricting Japanese penetration of the U.S. market and thus provided little benefit to the U.S. industry.

A major flaw in the design of the OMA as a policy instrument was its failure to take into account the inevitable shift of import market shares that would take place from Japan to Korea and Taiwan, to say nothing of stepped-up Japanese investments in the United States itself. (The recent recommendation by the International Trade Commission to the president concerning the OMA for stainless steel flatware explicitly recognizes the leakage factor in naming not only Japan as a proposed signatory but also Korea and Taiwan.) Imports of Japanese color television dropped by 17 percent to 2.23 million in 1977 from the 1976 level, but the shortfall was more than overcome by shipments from other countries representing principally pass-through points for Japanese production. Color imports from Taiwan totaled 462,300 in 177, up 94 percent from 1976; from Korea, 98,400, up 78 percent; and from Singapore, 14,100, up 416 percent.

An examination of the dollar value of imports of color television sets yields similar results. The dollar values of these imports in the first two months of 1978 were $83 million directly from Japan and another $26 million from other countries (Korea and Taiwan) serving Japanese firms as pass-through points. This total of $109 million compares to $95 million in the first two months of 1977, which was before the OMA was in effect and was a period when the Japanese were shipping heavily to beat the probable imposition of tariff or quota.

The U.S. government belatedly rectified this situation by signing similar import quota OMAs with Taiwan and Korea in February 1979. (U.S. firms with production facilities on Taiwan, such as RCA, were not enthusiastic about these OMAs because their imports were also affected.) As a result of these three OMAs, U.S.-based production by Japanese firms have been steadily increasing. From 750,000 sets produced in the United States in 1976, the sum increased to 1.2 million in 1977. This figure represented one of every six sets manufactured in the United States in 1977. By 1979 installed production capacity by Japanese firms in the United States was well over 2.5 million color television units. As a result of the increasingly high level of Japanese production in the United States and the decreasing level of Japan-originated imports, the U.S. government did not seek an extension of the OMA with Japan, which expired in June 1980. Yet new two-year OMAs were signed with Korea and Taiwan in July 1980 to continue restricting the flow of imports from those countries.

An oversight in the design of the OMA, which has undermined its effectiveness, is the definition of incomplete receivers by the Customs Office and the special trade negotiator, which has been easy to circumvent. The definition is such that a manufacturer could do all of the assembly work offshore except interconnecting certain nonchassis components such as tuners and yokes, and the import would qualify as an incomplete receiver as long as those components were not shipped in the same Customs entry as the chassis.

But the most serious dimension of the OMA, which requires reexamination, concerns the intended and actual beneficiary of the arrangement. We assume here that the intent of the OMA was to reinforce the competitive position of U.S.-based production, including American workers, plant facilities and equipment, and technology. Given the already subtantial offshore movement by all of the U.S. color television manufacturers, however, the OMA, even if it did not suffer from design and implementation flaws, would simply serve to reinforce the competitive position of foreign-based U.S. production over other foreign-based Japanese production. This strikes us as a difference without a distinction.

We would not level this criticism if there were some indication that the U.S. firms in the industry viewed the three-year respite as an opportunity to return to and revitalize their former U.S. production facilities, to invest in upgrading and retooling manufacturing techniques and processes, to redesign or reengineer the product or production system to achieve new efficiencies and cost savings, or to expend R&D funds on new or extended generations of television technology, such as the VTR. But there has been little evidence to this effect. In fact, in the first twelve months of the OMA's term, the only major change in the U.S. industry was Zenith's move to join the other U.S. manufacturers in low-wage production sites and a severe curtailment in its R&D expenditures and personnel.

With the pressure or incentive eliminated to cut labor costs, technological innovations in either process or product design rarely occur in offshore manufacturing operations. Typically the U.S. manufacturer enters a holding pattern regarding technological upgrading and innovation and eventually becomes locked into the existing state of the art. The OMA or any subsequent U.S. policy efforts to revitalize U.S. industry must pose a greater challenge, in the form of either incentives or penalties, to U.S. firms to enhance the competitiveness of their industry and employment.

Note

1. The actual figures have been compiled by the International Trade Commission. It is our estimate that of the 9 million sets sold in the United States in 1977, including Japanese-made sets, U.S. value added was probably no more than 30 percent.

7

Major Causes of
Decline in U.S. Industry

In many respects, the current problems of the U.S. color television industry can be traced back to its failure or inability to seize upon opportunities at strategic points over the past decade, particularly in response to the growing Japanese challenge. Such opportunities included countervailing expansion into Japanese and other world markets, aggressive commercialization of new-generation products, retention of advanced production in the United States through new investments in product-design adaptation and production engineering, and maintenance of full product lines. The timing and commitment required to realize these opportunities are as important as the opportunities themselves. In cases where the effort was made, it was often too little and/or too late.

Cutback in R&D Expenditures

In contrast to the persistent and aggressive technological advance of Japanese enterprises, U.S. firms have been reducing R&D expenditures and moving into lower-risk profit centers. This represents corporate philosophies stressing short-term earnings and cost reductions.

The U.S. television industry spent approximately 2.6 percent of sales on R&D in the past seven years while Japanese color television manufacturers average annual R&D outlays of 4.25 percent of sales. U.S. firms have cut back on basic research, and expenditures are limited largely to maintenance of existing product lines, with less and less going into developing new generations of products. The massive movement offshore by U.S. firms using state-of-the-art technology also indicates a reduction of expenditures to design and production engineer for the high-wage U.S. economy.[1]

Indicative of a U.S. industry-wide phenomenon of movement away from new-generation product development toward existing-product maintenance or improvement, Zenith discontinued its Research Department in September 1978, primarily to reduce costs; this department had been primarily concerned with long-term basic R&D work. After the release of several Research Department employees, a new department concerned with product development was set up, in which a number of research activities were reorganized. This realignment basically focused the activities of the remaining former research personnel into strengthening projects in an advanced stage of development; all research that is not product oriented has

113

been dropped. Similarly RCA until very recently had been restricting all R&D activity at its main laboratory in Princeton to existing-product improvement. And its four-year delay in putting into production its videotape disc system is reflective of the hesitancy of U.S. firms across a broad spectrum of industries to commit themselves to new-product development and production.

A major contributing factor to the retrenchment in R&D expenditures has been severe industry-wide price competition, which has characterized the U.S. market for the past several years. In Zenith's and RCA's battle for market-share supremacy, they have engaged in competitive pricing practices that have had a debilitating effect on their profits. As the other U.S. manufacturers have been forced to price their products extremely low to remain competitive, they too have suffered from poor profitability performance. Both RCA and GTE have been able to offset partially declining earnings, and even losses, in the sale of television and the loss of color television market shares through expanded sales of color television picture tubes to both U.S. and newly entrenched Japanese assemblers in the United States.

The industry-wide retrenchment from R&D and production upgrading commitments flows directly from the unsatisfactory profitability performance of the past several years. Faced with these financial difficulties, the U.S. color television manufacturers have uniformly reduced their R&D expenditures as one of the first steps to reduce costs. By comparison, the Japanese companies have maintained a much higher level of R&D expenditures without much difference in profitability from U.S. firms, and this is now paying off in substantial leads in the product cycle for new-generation television equipment.

Product Segment Relinquishment

U.S. color television manufacturers have further weakened their international competitive position while permitting the Japanese firms to strengthen their positions through a failure to maintain adequate product arrays. U.S. manufacturers can be faulted on several counts in this area. Some have released segments of product lines or relevant technology through licensing much too rapidly and extensively, and this has contributed to the rapid and successful takeover of production by Japanese enterprise. U.S. manufacturers have concentrated their production efforts on high-markup items, such as the larger television consoles, while either abandoning or allocating insufficient resources to the lower-markup product segments. This product relinquishment by U.S. firms has afforded Japanese manufacturers opportunities to preempt the lower end of product-line groups, such as portable television sets.

By developing strong production and marketing capabilities in segments relinquished by U.S. manufacturers, the Japanese firms have established beachheads from which to attack progressively those product segments in which U.S. firms are still competitive. In contrast to U.S. manufacturers, the Japanese have expended great efforts, which are reaping ample rewards, in maintaining a full array of products that dovetail and reinforce each other in their use of common componentry. The Japanese firms' full range of color television (and related consumer electronic products) allows them to move into an ever-widening range of U.S. market segments and thus put great competitive pressure on U.S. firms.

Potentially more detrimental to U.S. color television manufacturers than maintaining a limited array of existing products has been the relinquishment of new-product segments. At the same time they were sloughing off the mature or low-markup color television product segments, they were not moving into new-product areas as aggressively as were their Japanese competitors. Not only have Japanese manufacturers taken over substantial segments of the U.S. color television market (about 22 percent), they have also taken the lead in developing the new generations of consumer electronic products, such as the VTR. This again is a reflection of U.S. firms' failure to support high-risk, new-product development in what is likely to become a billion dollar a year market.

Quick-Return Mentality

A study of U.S. enterprises in the color television field indicates a growing aversion to take the technological risks needed to maintain market shares and international competitiveness. This is evidenced by the overall decline in the level of R&D expenditures and, in particular, in the research necessary to develop new-product generations and to retain competitive production methods in the high-wage U.S. economy. The corporate desire for quick returns at low risk has reinforced this lack of commitment to R&D and design engineering work, as well as contributed to the practice of technology sharing (licensing) in order to maintain corporate earnings without costly investment in research and capital plant.

These dimensions of what may be termed a quick-return, low-risk mentality, pervasive in a growing number of sectors of the U.S. economy, are having a critical effect on the erosion of U.S. color television manufacturers' technological base. An examination of the color television industry provides evidence of a movement by several of these firms into service industries at the expense of technological capabilities and a manufacturing orientation toward product segments involving relatively modest investment in RD&E (research, design, and engineering) and new plant and equipment relative to the time span and certainty of return on those products.

Effects of Currency Revaluation

It is significant to note the different signals to industry that prevail in Japan when faced with an appreciating currency, as compared to U.S. firms' reaction when the dollar depreciates in relative value. Japanese color television manufacturers have invested in the redesign of products and modernized industrial plants in order to offset the increasing price of exports and, to a lesser degree, to compete with the reduced prices of foreign imports. For U.S. firms, the effect of devaluations over the past several years has been to shield the firms from foreign competition and, in their eyes, to reduce the need to improve production efficiencies through expenditures in R&D and toward new plant and equipment. In the U.S. color television makers' markets, the new price advantage to a large degree has obviated these firms' need to improve productivity and product competitiveness in the near term. In short, the Japanese color television industry has thrived on adversity whereas the U.S. color television industry has been lulled into a state of declining resiliency and competitiveness.

It seems at first a paradox that the U.S. color television industry's share of the world market is declining despite progressive devaluation of the U.S. dollar and the price advantage the revaluation of currencies has given it over its major trading adversaries in Japan and Western Europe. In great part, the explanation of the paradox lies in technological erosion and lack of market aggressiveness of the U.S. color television manufacturers, which are no longer in a sufficiently strong position to take advantage of currency revaluations.

Effects of Technology Sharing

There is much evidence of a growing tendency among American firms to share highly competitive technology with foreign enterprise groups as a means for maintaining world market positions and global corporate earnings.[2] RCA, for example, received over $70 million in royalties from such sales in 1978, or 25 percent of its net income for that year. For some companies, international transfers of technology—either through relocation of production facilities or through licensing—have become a matter of corporate survival and part of their global strategy to maintain cost competitiveness in the U.S. and in foreign markets. The conventional wisdom has been that these technology exports were on balance beneficial to the U.S. economy and unavoidable in the sense that unless the U.S. firms moved or sold its technology abroad, it would lose market shares and suffer a net decline in earnings.

Yet technology-sharing arrangements place a heavy burden on U.S. enterprise in the aggregate to maintain the technological leads necessary to continue to meet foreign competition. When U.S. television manufacturers sold technology to Japanese firms, they intended to stay several steps ahead in technological capabilities. But the U.S. firms did not adequately assess the Japanese manufacturers' strong absorptive capacity for technology or their aggressive market-penetrating capabilities. As a consequence, the Japanese color television manufacturers are progressively displacing their former technology suppliers from their traditional markets.

Failure to Penetrate Foreign Markets

In a wide variety of industrial sectors, American companies have been loathe to make the necessary commitment of capital and time needed to create strong export programs, nor have they been willing to establish adequate servicing operations abroad for their products. In the consumer electronics industry, total sets exported by all U.S. firms reached a high of 410,000 units in 1973. In 1979 total U.S. industry exports (including those of U.S.-based Japanese firms) totaled only 375,000 units. Had the U.S. industry exploited foreign market opportunities more intensively during the 1960s when it actually had a technological lead (as the Japanese later demonstrated could be done), the substantial foothold gained by the Japanese in the U.S. market might have been precluded. Expanded exports could have lowered production cost and enhanced the industry's cash flow and earnings, thereby permitting investments in production modernization.

Until the early 1960s, Japan itself offered what should have been an attractive market for U.S.-brand color television sets, particularly the medium- to large-screen models, and at that time there were no restrictive barriers on imports into Japan. Color television sets in Japan were wholesaled at an average $150 higher than a U.S. model offering a larger and sharper picture. Despite advantages in circumstances, however, American firms, with the exception of Zenith, have never made any serious effort to penetrate the Japanese market.

Zenith took the initiative in the early 1960s, but observers have noted that its strategy was flawed by insufficient market research on how the Japanese distributorship system works. Reportedly it contracted with a large Japanese trading company to sell its sets. While excellent marketers of raw materials, some of these firms are indifferent sellers within the Japanese market of manufactured products, especially those requiring considerable after-sale service. In any event, Zenith's exported sets failed to reach any significant number of end consumers in Japan.

The International Trade Commission's 1977 Report to the President makes reference to the two unsuccessful attempts by Zenith to penetrate the Japanese market.[3] The ITC attributes Zenith's lack of success more to Japanese government intervention than to oversights or failures on Zenith's part. In the first instance, the Japanese government intervened and reportedly halted negotiations between Zenith and C. Itoh and Co. in the early 1960s for the export of U.S.-produced television receivers to Japan. The second effort, initiated in July 1972, was again thwarted by objections raised by a semiofficial Japanese agency regarding the technical characteristics of Zenith receivers. By February 1974 Zenith's management decided to give up its efforts to satisfy that agency. Zenith also alleges that various Japanese manufacturers control a large number of Japanese retail outlets, thus controlling the brands that these outlets are permitted to purchase and sell. The company reports that it was unable to place its sets in the retail stores.

It is not known on what grounds the Japanese government halted the negotiations or raised objections concerning the technical standards of Zenith sets (they may or may not have been legitimate), but what is common between the two reports is the decision by Zenith to market the products through a large trading company, C. Itoh, which turned out to be an inappropriate choice for selling consumer goods in Japan. The question can be raised as to whether other means of market penetration were adequately explored.

The example of Zenith underlines the importance of timely action, as well as commitment (in market research, technical adaptation, and managerial time), to succeed in exploiting new market opportunities when they arise. In fact, Zenith's second effort in 1972 may have been too late. It was in the late 1950s that the Japanese market was particularly vulnerable to imports. By the mid-1960s, Japanese production of color sets had rapidly increased, and from 1965 to 1970, production output nearly tripled every year while the rate of increase for U.S. manufacturers approximated 40 percent. Consequently Japanese color television producers, in keeping with the learning curve, were able to reduce their per-unit production cost at a much more accelerated rate than were U.S. firms. By 1970 the color television cost disadvantage initially suffered by the Japanese against U.S. manufacturers was clearly overcome.

Successful export programs require intensive research to yield the critical distinctions in consumer preferences and distributorship practices in a foreign country. U.S. television manufacturers have not been as assiduous as the Japanese in performing this task, even in the home market. For example, although GE introduced the first U.S. color portable set as early as 1965 (accompanied by a relatively unaggressive and unsustained marketing campaign), it was only some time after the low-cost and stylishly designed portables imported from Japan had achieved substantial market penetration that American companies began to broaden production beyond bulky, expensive, console models. More recently poor market research for home VTR and video disc systems reinforced U.S. firms' decisions to delay commercialization; Japanese companies, using more-accurate research, determined the existence of a significant market and commercialized this new-generation product. They now dominate the U.S. market for VTRs.

Inadequacies in Product Engineering
for World Markets

Even more costly and demanding than designing a product to meet different consumer tastes is the technical adaptation that must be done on product design and production engineering to meet various conditions and standards in export markets; yet the potential rewards can be great in terms of increased world market shares. In a television receiver, two important variables determine the set's technical suitability in different markets. The first variable is the ability of the set to receive more than one transmission frequency. Different frequency banks are used by different countries for television transmission, and for one set to be usable in a variety of countries, it must feature a special tuner that adjusts to the particular frequency.

The second variable is the ability of a set to adjust to the various power-supply systems used in different countries. This ability requires the set's transformer to be equipped with multiple windings, controlled by a switch that turns the set on to the correct voltage. A further complication, whose solution requires the design of an entirely different set, is that among European countries, two different systems or techniques for color picture transmission have been adopted, neither of them compatible with the U.S. color television system. In addition, safety and environmental regulations for television receivers, such as the permissible levels of radiation emission, vary widely among countries.

Clearly the technical adaptations necessary to design and manufacture a television set that can meet the requirements of a variety of export markets are substantial and therefore costly. U.S. firms have felt that the profit margins achievable in export markets do not justify the investment. Japanese firms, on the other hand, consonant with their aggressive export tendencies, have designed the product and production system so as to ensure compatibility with these myriad technical demands. To avoid reducing volume, and thereby lose expanding economies of scale in their manufacture, a variety of adaptations is routinely incorporated into Japanese-made sets. In cases where the market size justifies a separate production run, such as in the United States, technical features that are necessary only for that market are incorporated into the set. Yet most of the Japanese models on the U.S. market can be easily adjusted to operate in other countries that have different transmission and power-supply systems.

There is no indication that U.S. firms have undertaken the R&D needed to incorporate this market versatility in the technical standards of their sets, although they may have made the effort and failed, nevertheless, to produce a commercial product. There is ample evidence, however, that U.S. industry does have the capability to redesign products and production systems so that its exports are compatible in different markets with varying technical standards. GE is a good case in point, although its expertise in this area has not been applied to color television manufacture but rather, to the production of a numerical control system. Until 1972 GE manufactured numerical control equipment in the United States, Italy, and Great Britain, in cooperation with the Hawker Siddeley Group, Ltd. Rather than make substantial investments in expensive inspection and quality-control machinery in all three plants, GE shifted all production to its plant in Richmond, Virginia, despite the fact that 40 percent of the company's $50 million in annual sales of numerical controls go to Europe. This move necessitated the adaption of the equipment to the technical needs of foreign markets. GE has developed a numerical control system that is usable in both metric and English measures and has also designed the machines necessary to accommodate the wide differences in voltage among European countries.

Part of the explanation for the willingness of Japanese firms to undertake technical adjustments, in contrast to U.S. firms, may be traced to wage differentials for technical support personnel in Japan as compared to the United States. The Japanese labor market is structured so that large numbers of technically qualified and often university-trained personnel typically enter Japanese firms at relatively low salaries and are kept at a low earnings level for extended periods, a distinct advantage in this regard.

American firms have forfeited not only the opportunity to expand markets but also the opportunity to expand product lines; again the Japanese have benefited from this action. Marketing efforts by U.S. firms tend to push U.S. consumers as close as possible to the upper end of any product line, where the profit margins are generally higher. The relative vacuum created at the lower end is rapidly filled by competitive imports. Rather than attempt to regain lost market segments, several U.S. industries find it in their interest to cede this end of a domestic product line to Japanese and other competitors. For example, manufacturers of motorcycles gave up trying to compete in the field of light motorcycles and concentrated efforts on larger, and more-profitable, bikes. Ball-bearing producers relinquished the high-volume, low-technology end of their markets to the European and Japanese. The Xerox Corporation quit production of the nonautomated end of the copier market (fewer than twenty copies per minute).

Underlying the decision to relinquish product segments to foreign producers is the assumption that the U.S. manufacturer is capable of retaining firm control over the higher segments of the product line. As we are witnessing today in, for example, color television, copiers, and automobiles, this estimation of U.S. capability is grossly exaggerated. It also overlooks the fact that although the Japanese may begin at the low end of a product line, they also begin at such high volume that earnings are sufficient to permit the development and use of highly specialized machine tools. Using more-efficient equipment than their competitors, they are able to move rapidly up the product line to the point where they pose strong competition to U.S. producers in all segments of the market.

Japanese firms were able to finance their swift technological advances in consumer electronics with the earnings generated from large production volumes. In quick succession, they moved from transistor radios, to tape recorders, to black-and-white television. Once the Japanese achieved a certain share of the U.S. market for each of these products, the U.S. producers considered it less and less worthwhile to invest in maintaining this market and did not put up a strong competitive struggle against the Japanese and others. As a consequence, the U.S. industry is now squeezed from both ends of the product line. The Japanese have not only assumed a large and growing portion of the U.S. color television market; they are also preempting the new generation of VTR products, which have already passed $3 billion annually.

Notes

1. In this regard the exports of the Foxboro Corporation, a leading U.S. designer and manufacturer of automated tooling, now account for over half of its sales, as compared to about 20 percent a decade ago. While this fact could reflect unrelated considerations, such as a change in Foxboro's marketing thrust, it would still appear to indicate a relative decline in U.S. automation. Based upon remarks by a Foxboro official at the annual meeting of the American Association for the Advancement of Science, Houston, Texas, January 4, 1979. The huge lead that Japanese industry, in aggregate, has over all other nations in the use of robotics is another reflection of relative commitments to design engineer for advanced production methods.

2. This tendency is documented and analyzed in Jack Baranson, *Technology and the Multinationals* (Lexington, Mass.: Lexington Books, D.C. Heath and Co., 1978).

3. *Television Receivers, Color and Monochrome, Assembled or Not Assembled, Finished or Not Finished, and Subassemblies Thereof* (Washington, D.C.: International Trade Commission, March 1977), p. A-77.

Part IV
Sources of Japanese Competitiveness in Consumer-Electronics Industries

Product Leadership

Technical and Commercial Strategies

The corporate policies and strategies that Japanese consumer electronics firms have been pursuing place them in a strong position to dominate this industry. Their strong commitment to product and process R&D and their aggressiveness in commercializing new products, coupled with sustained support of high-risk and delayed-return investments, have helped them attain the leading position they now hold in consumer electronics. The recent effort by General Electric to join forces with Hitachi in the consumer electronics field was tacit recognition of the technological lead Japanese firms have attained; Hitachi was to provide the technology in the proposed joint venture. This leadership position is reinforced by the long-term views most Japanese take toward their business operations, their aggressive policies for global market penetration, and the collaborative relationship between Japanese government and industry.

Another major strength of Japanese industry that contributes to its international competitiveness has been, and continues to be, its well-integrated and highly responsive pyramid of subcontracting enterprises. These medium to small-size firms (employing anywhere from several hundred to a dozen or fewer people) supply the myriad of components and parts required by manufacturers of consumer electronic products. Two features of these subcontracting pyramids are highly supportive of the efficiency and competitiveness of Japanese industry. One is that these firms are highly responsive to the endless design and engineering changes that a dynamic industry requires. (One of the difficulties Japanese firms have in the United States is a much lower and less-adequate level of responsiveness among U.S. component and parts suppliers, according to several Japanese plant managers interviewed in Japan and in California.) Japanese supplier firms are provided the technical liaison and the financial support necessary to redesign parts and components and to upgrade or expand installed plant and equipment. A second supportive factor is that subcontracting firms serve as shock absorbers in economic cycles of expansion and downturn, thereby making possible the advantageous features of life employment in the larger firms.

In examining the leadership position of Japanese firms in the consumer electronics industry, the focus should not be restricted to color television.

Television receivers and VTRs constitute only part of a larger involvement in the field of consumer electronics and, in many cases, industrial electronics and electronics in general. These firms develop a commonality of advanced technology among a wide range of consumer and industrial products by establishing a commonality of componentry and manufacturing techniques among these products. In this fashion, the Japanese consumer electronics firms enjoy substantial economies of scale in R&D and in component manufacturing, while also enjoying a broad exposure in the consumer electronics marketplace, thus ensuring steady and sizable cash flows for future capital investment.

The international competitiveness of the Japanese firms has been greatly enhanced by their ability to coordinate tightly the R&D, commercialization, and product-upgrading functions. The R&D work that Japanese color television manufacturers perform is quickly moved into the commercialization process, and frequently the same R&D results that generate a new product can be dovetailed into product upgrading. (Commercialization refers to the process by which R&D work on new products is translated into the manufacturing of these products for the marketplace. Product upgrading refers to the process by which previously commercialized products are improved through product or production process design changes.) Indeed it is difficult to distinguish between commercialization and product upgrading efforts of Japanese firms. These firms offer a broad and deep array of consumer electronics products that are constantly evolving up the technology scale, and it is hard to pinpoint when a product moves from the commercialization phase to the upgrading phase.

Yet in general, Japanese firms in the past have not been in the forefront of groundbreaking R&D work for consumer electronics. Their strength has been in taking early prototypes developed by the R&D work of others and successfully commercializing it through rapid, continuous, and incremental improvements in the basic technology, with a constant eye on the marketplace. In performing this task, the Japanese firms have been the pacesetters. In terms of developing next-generation technology, several Japanese government and industry officials have indicated Japan's relative weakness in this area due to social, cultural, and historical factors.[1] But while willing to admit this, the Japanese firms are also attempting to strengthen their technical capabilities in this area. And any lack of success may not threaten their leadership in consumer electronics. The increasingly rapid diffusion of technology today means that the Japanese firms can obtain advanced foreign technology far upstream and then begin commercialization.

Any prediction of the Japanese industry's future leadership in consumer electronics should be qualified by indicating three variables. First, the Japanese industry's present major international competitors may be able to challenge the Japanese firms' leadership position, if not across the board then in selected product categories. The two major U.S. firms, RCA and Zenith, still retain substantial competitive capabilities, as well as significant U.S. market shares. In its recent video disc work, RCA has shown a renewed commitment to consumer electronics. Similarly N.V. Philips of the Netherlands and other European firms, such as West Germany's Grundig, remain strong international competitors. Second, the emergence of regional manufacturers in Southeast Asia, China, and Latin America, where advantages of low-cost labor and government support are present, represents a threat to the Japanese volume production and marketing strategy conducted on a global basis. Third, the nature of the consumer electronics industry is evolving into areas where Japanese industry does not yet enjoy an uncontested leadership position, such as in semiconductors and fiber optics.

R&D Performed by Japanese Firms

Average expenditures by Japanese manufacturers of consumer electronics products for all categories of R&D (development, applied and what little basic research, if any, that they do) exceed U.S. firms' R&D expenditures by 50 percent. In 1978 the weighted average of R&D as a percentage of sales for the four major U.S. color television manufacturers was 2.3 percent; for five Japanese color television manufacturers (Hitachi, Matsushita, Sanyo, Sony, and Toshiba) the average was 3.5 percent, up from 3.2 percent in 1977.

It has been observed generally that Japanese consumer electronics firms by and large have relied upon foreign manufacturers, particularly U.S. firms, to develop the basic technology and often the first commercial prototype, which they then adapt, improve, and commercialize. Whereas U.S. firms typically have emphasized basic R&D and new-product development, Japanese firms have concentrated on product upgrading and improving manufacturing technology. Until recently the importing of foreign technology under licensing agreements has afforded Japanese firms a relatively cheap way of adding new product lines.

The following three cases selected at random provide evidence of the dependence of Japanese color television firms on basic R&D performed by foreign firms. First, New Nippon Electric signed a five-year patent licensing and technical know-how contract in 1979 with the U.S. firm Kloss Video Corporation for production of a unique, enlarged color television screening system. A second example is that of Sony, which entered into a cross-licensing arrangement in 1979 with N.V. Philips primarily to gain access to the latter's advanced optical video disc technology. A third case involves Sanyo, Toshiba, Sharp, and Matsushita, which have begun utilizing voice-synthesis technology originally developed by Texas Instruments in an increasingly wide range of consumer electronics products, such as color televisions, clocks, and digital height meters. Until products actually appear in the marketplace, the acquisition of foreign technology by Japanese firms may be purely a protective measure, of course.

The Japanese consumer electronics industry also relies on government and university laboratories, primarily for basic research leading to new-product conceptualization and development. Government laboratories involved in consumer electronics-related projects, particularly NHK, make the results of their work freely available to Japanese firms and work closely with them on specific projects.

The laboratories of several Japanese universities engage in basic R&D work that has application to consumer electronics. This work has been made freely available to the industry through university-to-industry channels or by way of the Japanese government. Additionally university laboratories may be commissioned by Japanese firms to perform R&D work. Recent examples of such work that has direct application to the consumer electronics field include a new vertical magnetizing recording disc developed at the University of Sendai's Research Institute of Electrical Communication, which could enable a recorder-reproducer to work ten times longer than present models, and a device incorporating laser hologram technology, developed at the University of Tokyo's Institute of Industrial Science, which can be attached to a television camera and receiving set to produce three-dimensional stereoscopic pictures.

The comparative advantage of Japanese technical personnel derives in part from its educational system, which brings a large number of people to a median level of technical skills and craftsmanship and is coupled with the culturally induced characteristic of highly motivated teamwork. These characteristics have contributed to the high levels of productivity and near-zero defect reliability in Texas Instruments' plant in Japan (Hiji Works). The leading Japanese firms are able to offer young engineers interesting and challenging work in a wide range of product-design engineering assignments. This contrasts dramatically with the experience of a young American engineer we interviewed who quit Motorola after six frustrating years of management unreceptiveness to innovative initiatives by staff engineers.

The Japanese consumer electronics industry acknowledges its lack of basic R&D for next-generation technology and is now considering concerted efforts to overcome this deficiency. The recent reordering of Matsushita's technological priorities is indicative of this new direction. Over the years Matsushita has moved from being a company with near-total reliance on foreign technology to one that ranks second to none in using innovative technology in consumer electronics production. Previously whenever a competing consumer appliance company brought out a new product, Matsushita would rush to bring out a similar one. By selling its product for less and advertising more, the firm often outsold its rivals in the lucrative domestic market. Two years ago, however, the firm launched a major drive to upgrade its R&D activities, which further enhanced its position as Japan's top manufacturer of consumer electronics. The company now spends between 4 and 5 percent of its earnings on R&D. As part of the drive to upgrade research efforts, Matsushita further consolidated the activities of its twenty-three research laboratories, and management has called for shorter lead times on new-product development.

A further example of the growing commitment to doing more basic, long-term R&D work by Japanese firms is evident in a recent decision by Sanyo to establish a very large-scale integrated circuits (VLSI) research center. This research center, the focal point of a three-year project aimed at introducing VLSIs into home electrical appliances, will be equipped with the latest electron beam exposure units, imported from the United States, in order to facilitate the integration of VLSIs into consumer electronics products. Initial investment was set at $55 million.

Product and Process Engineering

A major strength of the Japanese consumer electronics equipment manufacturing firms lies in the great emphasis they place on production process development and the related adjustments in product designs that contribute to cost-effective, high-quality production. The twin goals that Japanese color television manufacturers have been striving for in their constant refinement of product and process engineering have been a decrease in unit costs and a reduction of defect percentages (moving to zero-defect production). Closely linked to these production goals, and flowing from them, has been a constant concern for product quality and reliability. Japanese manufacturers perceive a mutually reinforcing relationship between cost-efficient production and the upgrading of product design.

To reap the full advantage of this relationship, Japanese firms closely coordinate production process development and design engineering for products. Simultaneous and complementary changes in product designs and production systems result from a close coordination between the product design and production engineering departments and are part of the overall integration of different departments in a Japanese firm. The same applies to components divisions, which also contribute to product-and-process engineering discussions.

A major emphasis in product upgrading by Japanese firms has been upon reducing the number of components in a given product. This contemporary reduction, combined with advanced production methods, results in lower manufacturing costs and improved product quality and reliability. The significant reduction of componentry that has occurred in Japanese color televisions has been achieved through an increased utilization of ICs (integrated circuits) and LSIs (large-scale integrated circuits). For example, at Sanyo's Gifu Factory, which manufactures twenty-inch color televisions, 2,334 parts were required for the manufacture of one set in 1970; by 1976, with the introduction of LSI componentry, the required parts had been reduced to 1,006.

In terms of production process development, Japanese firms have been most concerned with increasing their levels of automation. The upgrading of products through the increased use of ICs and microprocessors has allowed for rapid advances in automation because these components lend themselves to easy automatic insertion. At present, for example, automatic insertion equipment accounts for over 75 percent of the components inserted in printed circuit boards by Japanese color television firms. In the Sanyo color television plant at Gifu, set assembly is also fully automated. The plant has three sets of automatic insert machines manufactured by Universal in the United States and ten sets of Japanese-made machines, including Matsushita's advanced PANA-SERT.

The close relationship between production process development in the form of increased automation and product design and upgrading in the form of component reduction through ICs is one in which an advance in one function often stimulates or reinforces an advance in the other. In this sense, a reduction of componentry allows for increased levels of automated insertion and soldering processes, and automated assembly and processing decreases the defect rate and enhances the reliability performance of products. A Japanese government agency official estimated that the defect ratio for color television sets manufactured in Japan in 1979 was 0.4 percent, as compared to 5 percent for U.S. sets.

Japanese commitment to automation is seen in the number of industrial robots in operation in Japan. The country has 13,000 of the world's 17,500 industrial robots; the U.S. has 2,500 (however, Japan includes in its definition of robots a wide range of hand manipulators, which are not included in the U.S. definition). Japan has seventy companies developing new robots, as compared to twenty-seven firms in the United States. Further, a $50 million Japanese research program aims at factories that are operated completely by robots.

This commitment to automation is part of the broader commitment by Japanese industry to capital investment as the best means of enhancing competitiveness.[2] Some Japanese firms still endeavor to maintain ten-year scrap-and-rebuild plans for their production facilities. Matsushita, for example, in its 1980 investment plan, announced extensive scrap-and-rebuild programs, requiring a doubling of plant and equipment investment over the previous year (40 billion yen versus 23 billion yen in fiscal 1979). Sanyo announced capital expenditures of 51 billion yen for fiscal 1980 in order to install new production facilities and expand existing plants. Sanyo's investment outlays for that year emphasized work on VLSIs, metal-oxide semiconductors, and LSIs.

Vertical Component Integration and
Horizontal Product Spread

Central to the Japanese consumer electronic firms' evolving leadership in this industry has been the generally high degree of vertical integration and broad horizontal range of product development and commercialization that has characterized these firms' activities. These two aspects of Japanese color television producers, which appear in greater or lesser degrees in individual companies, are mutually reinforcing. Throughout the broad range of products that a Japanese firm may manufacture is an increasingly high degree of commonality in higher-technology componentry, which thus serves as an assured outlet for high-volume production of these components. Although the ability to produce a high volume of componentry results in lowered manufacturing costs and thus keeps the price of final products competitive, the broad array of products offered by a Japanese firm serves as a hedge against heavy dependence on one product for overall corporate performance, as well as increasing the overall sales generation potential. (During several interviews with U.S. and Japanese sources knowledgeable about the industry, the opinion was expressed that the long-range goal of Japanese consumer electronics firms is to become worldwide suppliers of high-technology componentry, thus retaining advanced-technology capabilities while farming out lower-technology component and parts assembly and manufacture to nonaffiliated firms in and out of Japan.)

The in-house production of semiconductor components has become characteristic among Japanese color television and VTR manufacturers, and this tendency has far-reaching implications in terms of aggressive leadership in product dynamics and cost-effectiveness. Various-sized integrated circuits increasingly are appearing in a broad range of products from Japanese consumer electronics firms. Among the five largest Japanese semiconductor manufacturers, which account for 66 percent of total Japanese integrated circuit production, are Hitachi, Toshiba, and Matsushita. Other large manufacturers include Sanyo, Sony, and Sharp. All of these firms are vertically integrated end users, with Sanyo and Sony apparently using most of their semiconductor output in-house.

By developing their supply of semiconductors internally for their finished products, Japanese consumer electronics firms are able to coordinate the design of these components and the products that will use them through integrated planning procedures, an advantage not enjoyed to a significant degree by most U.S. competitors. Japan has become an expanding source of semiconductors for the U.S. consumer electronics industry, and U.S. firms that have continued to procure their semiconductors from U.S. supplier industries have run into difficulties. One reason is that the U.S. semiconductor industry focuses its production for end use on the computer and telecommunications field. As a consequence, the U.S. semiconductor industry has not been overly responsive to the U.S. consumer electronics industry's semiconductor requirements. Although RCA does maintain a significant integrated circuit production operation and Zenith has a limited capacity for the manufacture of microelectronic components, these two firms' semiconductor operations are not as closely integrated with their product design and manufacturing operations as those of Japanese firms. Thus the Japanese firms enjoy a substantial comparative advantage in this area over their U.S. competitors.

With the development of the all-solid-state receiver, semiconductor technology has facilitated product innovation in video electronics. For example, several Japanese color television firms are in the preliminary stages of the commercialization of voice-synthesis systems utilizing microprocessors. Sharp has developed a voice-activated remote-control device that applies voice-recognition techniques to color-in-color, or dual-screen color, television and to a calculator. Matsushita has announced the development of a voice-activated color television, clock radio, and scale. Sanyo recently demonstrated a speech-recognition unit as a remote-control device that uses an eight-bit microprocessor; the unit responds to oral commands for activating a color television, a VTR, a radio cassette, an electric fan, and even tap water.

The examples of voice-synthesis technology used in a variety of consumer electronics products is illustrative of how Japanese firms dovetail a distinct technological development, most often in the form of componentry, into a wide range of consumer products. Thus while minimizing R&D and component manufacturing costs, the Japanese color television firms are able to offer a broad horizontal range of products. Matsushita, for example, spun off four distinct products from pulse code modulation (PCM) technology developed in 1978: a digital audio disc system, an optical-type digital audio disc system, a PCM recording processor, and a fixed head digital audio tape recorder. These four items were a mere fraction of the 540 introductions, or new-product developments, that Matsushita announced in 1978. An additional example of this Japanese color television firm phenomenon of spinning off technology into new products is evident in Sony's recent introduction of a television-style monitor for use with home VTRs, multiplex broadcasting, and home-information systems;

the monitor is based on Trinitron tube technology, an earlier Sony development that has been undergoing constant refinement (most recently in terms of reliability and quality through the introduction of a peak current equalizer system). Sony intends all this video equipment to create demand through an interrelated, multiplier effect. Sony has recently attempted to promote a new video projector that can be used with VTRs or video disc systems. Thus a major reason why Japanese firms have developed and promoted a broad array of related consumer products is that in many cases the purchase of one product leads to the purchase of another, related product.

Response to Global Market Opportunities

In October 1979 Toshiba demonstrated five new product innovations at the Japan Electronics Show in Osaka. One, the voice sensor, was a color television set with a voice-activated remote-control device. A second item was a color television set that can display four different channels simultaneously on one screen, with an earphone for sound selection. Televislide, Toshiba's third new product, screens negative or positive 35-millimeter photographs and can be used to compile video albums when connected to a VTR. The fourth new product demonstrated at Osaka, the telecalculator, is a microcomputer built into a television set that performs arithmetic tasks and offers dates through a perpetual calendar memory. The fifth Toshiba product on display was an audio-video synthetic system, which combines and controls a color television, VTR, record player, and microcomputer; it can be used for telephone answering and recording messages, recording television programs, serving as a wake-up alarm, and automatically turning off appliances not in use.

These innovations reflect an aggressive policy of Japanese consumer electronics firms to be among the forerunners in new market areas. Although Japanese firms may still rely in part on U.S. firms for the basic R&D in such areas as computers or voice synthesis, once they obtain the basic technology, the Japanese firms move rapidly to develop a prototype model for the consumer market, or, if demand is determined to be sufficient, they move directly into production. This policy incurs the obvious risks of sunken R&D and tooling costs prior to full demonstration of market potential. Yet if this policy is pursued over a sufficiently broad range of potential new consumer products, then the negative effect of individual product failures is minimized. The result of such policies is that these firms further enhance their chances for leadership in consumer electronics.

Some examples of Japanese consumer electronics firms' positioning themselves for a particular new market opportunity are instructive. The direct-to-home satellite antenna receiver is a case where several Japanese color television manufacturers are well prepared to exploit what may become a major worldwide market in the 1980s. Japan may be the first nation to deploy an operational satellite-to-home television broadcasting system. The concept has been undergoing field trials in Japan since July 1978, and the NHK government laboratory has taken the lead, in close cooperation with Japanese consumer electronics firms, in developing this concept. The potential of these television receivers worldwide represents the type of export market Japanese industry requires. In fact, in April 1980 the United States just missed witnessing the introduction of subscription television services by satellite when Comsat and Sears discontinued talks on establishing a joint venture in this area. Should this market develop, Japanese color television manufacturers such as Mitsubishi, Nippon Electric Co., and Sony will be at least one important step ahead of their U.S. counterparts because all have manufactured prototype small-dish antennas that can be placed indoors by a window and used for direct reception of satellite television broadcasts.

Another area where Japanese firms have anticipated an evolving worldwide market involves multiplex broadcasting. Multiplex broadcasting is a transmission system that allows for several information streams to be broadcast on one channel. This system can be used, for example, for transmitting still images on a standard television screen at a slow or rapid speed for varying effects; it can also be used in broadcasting foreign-language translations and programs. Multiplex broadcasting is becoming increasingly prevalent in Japan, and as a result 14 percent of the total domestic television shipments in 1979 contained built-in sound multiplex receivers. It was estimated that such color televisions shipped in 1980 would be about 40 percent, and for 1981 the total was estimated at 60 percent.

A more immediate example of positioning by Japanese firms for new market opportunities is seen in the fact that they are acquiring both optical and stylus video disc technology, the two major options in this field. Because the standard for this new product has not yet emerged, firms such as Hitachi, Sony, Toshiba, Mitsubishi, and Sharp are developing both types of systems, either through in-house technology or through licensing arrangements, in order to be able to exploit the market that is expected to develop rapidly once a system standard has been chosen.

At present, the consumer electronics industry is undergoing a major evolution involving the integration of advanced technologies that originated in industrial electronics. Although such adaptations have not been uncommon in the past, a significant degree of difference between past and present rates is found in the speed and frequency with which these adaptations are now occurring. The Japanese speak of a coming information- and communications-oriented world and, through concerted public and private efforts, intend to be major suppliers of information and communications equipment and services.

Computer technology is in the forefront of industrial technologies that are altering the state of the consumer electronics industry. Yet applications of other industrial technologies—particularly related to the telecommunications field (for example, fiber optics, digital electronics, and lasers)—are also beginning to appear more frequently in the consumer electronics industry. Although U.S. firms now generally enjoy a leadership position in industrial electronics technologies, it remains to be seen whether they can be as effective in the horizontal-product spread as Japanese firms have been.

With the increasing inflow of advanced electronics technology, the consumer electronics industry is witnessing a transition from passive, single-purpose products such as television, tape recorders, and radios to technologically advanced active systems involving a range of interrelated products. At the lower end of this active technology spectrum, a VTR is part of a system that requires a television and a home-movie camera in order to take full advantage of the product's capability; at the higher end of the product spectrum are the current prototype developments of computer-oriented home systems, designed to operate automatically TV-VTR units and serve as answering services and assist in a variety of other household chores, including drawing up family budgets. The success of these systems in the consumer marketplace will be contingent on aggressive marketing, decreasing production costs, and timely response to emerging consumer demand.

The evolution in consumer electronics to complex, integrated systems can be seen in prototype trials of these systems that are being conducted in both Japan and in the United States. In Higashi-Ikoma, Japan, a two-way audiovisual communications system is under evaluation by government and industry. Called Hi-Ovis (highly interactive optical visual information system), it provides a host of educational, leisure, social, and work services. Each of the 158 participating households has a camera, television terminal controller, keyboard, and microphone. Roughly 11,000 fiber-optic splices, strung along existing telephone and power lines, connect the participants. Hi-Ovis may represent the beginning of the transition to a new service-oriented society.

In 1974, in Columbus, Ohio, Warner Communications put its Qube system in operation on a test basis. Qube is centered around an interactive, or two-way, television set in each participant's home. By means of the set, the participant is able to vote in national or local referendums, shop in stores, book an airline flight, or pick up the mail, as well as watch regular television programming. Similarly, in the mid-1970s, in Jonathan, Maine, a two-way, interactive cable television service was installed to provide shopping, education, home security, information retrieval, opinion polling, and other services to town residents on an experimental basis. The project was sponsored by the Department of Housing and Urban Development, in cooperation with Community Information Systems, Inc., a cable television research and consulting firm.

The trend toward complex, active systems, which are part audio, part visual, part computer, and part telecommunications, is causing an increased blurring of the traditional roles of home, office, entertainment, and educational products. Thus market opportunities are arising for electronics firms that traditionally have not been involved in the consumer marketplace. U.S. industrial electronics firms could be represented in this evolving new consumer marketplace if they felt consumer electronics was a viable business opportunity. Burroughs, IBM, and Tektronix, as well as RCA, are heavily committed to R&D work for flat-screen television. IBM is moving into the video disc field by providing technology and manufacturing capability to Discovision, a firm in which IBM has 50 percent ownership with MCA. IBM's primary interest in video discs lies in their computer application as data-storage devices. The home computer marketplace, at present dominated by U.S. firms, is characterized by a diversity of U.S. industries, including Hewlett-Packard, Tandy Corporation, Apple Computer, Texas Instruments, Warner Communications, and Mattel.

A major question is whether the larger U.S. firms have the aggressiveness needed to commercialize such new systems and whether the smaller, highly innovative U.S. firms have the resources to do the same. This should be contrasted to the Japanese network of firms and government, which allows for a rapid and significant commitment to a new product area once the commercial potential is evident.

Notes

1. See also the Japanese publication *Journal of the Electronics Industry* (August 1979):37, for a discussion of this situation.

2. In a recent *Fortune* article, May 5, 1980, p. 196, Japanese manufacturers in the aggregate were identified as the highest reinvestors as a percentage of their output among major industrialized nations: 26.5 percent over the 1970 to 1977 period. U.S. manufacturers reinvested a meager 9.6 percent of their output during this period.

9

The Importance of Foreign Markets

There are marked differences between the importance that U.S. and Japanese firms assign to exploiting foreign market opportunities and the difficulties and risks each are willing to face in securing access to those markets. Generally Japanese firms have been much more interested and aggressive in pursuing these opportunities and taking these risks.

Overview of U.S. and Japanese Foreign Involvements

United States

The U.S. consumer electronics market is the world's largest and least protected, highly attractive to foreign and domestic producers alike. Inherently this situation provides an advantage to foreign firms wishing to export, for there is no other comparable single export market for U.S. firms to exploit. This point is not trivial; were it not for the size, sophistication, and accessibility of the U.S. market, Japanese production of VTRs and video discs would probably have been set back for years. With the U.S. market closed, Japanese consumer electronics firms would have been denied a major outlet for the volumes of production critical to their corporate strategy. Unlike their U.S. counterparts, however, the Japanese color television manufacturers have not been content to rely on one or even two markets. Less than one-third of the value of all Japanese consumer electronics exports went to the United States in 1978, although the percentage was higher (about one-half) for VTRs. While most U.S. color television firms concentrate their marketing activities in the United States, the Japanese view every country as a potential market.

Western Europe

In terms of size and sophistication, Western Europe offers the world's second most important consumer electronics market. Color television sales in 1980 were expected to reach 10 million units, about the same level as in the

United States. Sales have grown only moderately in recent years, but because the level of color television saturation in Europe is relatively low (especially in France, where it has been estimated at 33 to 39 percent) new demand is expected. VTR sales have been brisk, especially in West Germany, Britain, and France. West German demand alone was predicted to reach 300,000 units in 1980.

The European color television market, however, has been less accessible than its U.S. counterpart to foreign producers. Imports into the European Economic Community, the bulk of the European market, are discouraged at two levels. At the Community level, importers face the common external tariff of 14 percent ad-valorem and value-added taxes, ranging from 11 to 33 percent. At the national level, importers face a host of other restrictions, primarily quantitative. Japanese producers, for instance, have been obliged to accept a voluntary export restraint on color televisions to Britain, and annual negotiations between the electronics industry associations of France and Japan have reduced Japanese color television imports into France to 80,000 per year.

Access to the European color television market is further restricted by the nature of the broadcasting system, PAL, and by PAL's licensing agent, AEG Telefunken. (France, to make matters more difficult, operates on a separate broadcasting system, SECAM.) Telefunken initially refused to license Japanese firms wishing to produce color televisions compatible with the PAL systems; eleven Japanese firms now are licensed, but their production is restricted. Japanese licensees, for example, are banned in West Germany from marketing color televisions that are twenty-two inches or larger and that are made outside the EEC.

As a result of these restrictions, the European color television market has become largely self-sufficient. The Japanese do export to this market, but their export level is sharply limited; U.S. imports are virtually nonexistent. But just as they have done in the U.S. market, the Japanese have managed to circumvent export restrictions by switching to local-based production. Five Japanese firms now produce color televisions for the European market from British-based plants: Sony, Matsushita, Toshiba, Mitsubishi, and Hitachi (the last three having started production only within the past two years). Sony, Matsushita, and Mitsubishi each operates subsidiaries in Britain, and Toshiba and Hitachi participate in joint ventures: Toshiba with Rank Radio International and Hitachi with General Electric Corporation (not related to the U.S. firm GE).

British-based Japanese manufacturers produced 575,000 color televisions in 1979, twice as many as in 1978. Sony, in 1968 the first to locate in Britain, was also the first to export from Britain to West Germany. Toshiba recently became the second. While continuing to supply the German market with small-screen color televisions (fourteen inches or less) from Japan, Toshiba now sends larger models, including new twenty-two- and twenty-six-inch sets, from its British plant to that market, thereby circumventing PAL licensing restrictions on Japanese producers.

Japanese investment in European color television production is not limited to Britain. In Italy, Sanyo has increased its holdings in Emerson, a local color television manufacturer, to about 30 percent and may take full control, while Hitachi and A. Zanussi, another Italian color television firm, recently entered into a technical exchange agreement, a possible prelude to a joint venture. Sanyo also makes color televisions in Spain.

Japanese firms are pursuing a similar expansionist strategy in Europe for color television tubes. Exports have increased, apparently at the expense of U.S. producers. And parallelling the increase in sales of larger-sized Japanese color television in Europe (from U.K.-sited plants), Japanese consumer electronics firms now plan to supply the European market with their tubes for large-screen color televisions, previously the preserve of Philips and three other European firms. Hitachi, meanwhile, which already exports 50,000 to 100,000 tubes to Europe annually, is contributing technical work to a unique, joint public-private venture in Finland designed to produce 300,000 tubes per year for export to Europe and Africa.

U.S. manufacturers, on the other hand, are apparently withdrawing from the European color television market. GTE, the only U.S. firm with significant European holdings, was recently forced to sell two subsidiaries, Saba and Videon, at a loss. Saba, which makes televisions, audio equipment, radios and VTRs, has an 8 percent share of the West German color television market. Videon makes parts.

The French firm Thomson-Brandt, which purchased Saba and Videon from GTE, is now negotiating for control of West Germany's Nordermande as part of a trend toward consolidation among European producers. Philips is seeking full control of Pye Ltd.

Unlike the color television market, the European market for VTRs and video discs operates relatively free of restriction. As a result, it is fast becoming a battleground for supremacy among the European and Japanese producers of these advanced video products. Evidence suggests that after ignoring the European market for years while establishing a base in the United States, the Japanese industry is now doing very well, even in Germany, the home base of Grundig, one of its major European competitors. Imports into Britain and West Germany in the first five months of 1979 increased five times over the same period the year before, to about 55,000 each, while French imports jumped from 2,600 to more than 30,000. In response to the Japanese challenge, West Germany's Copyright Committee has requested that Japanese VTRs remain subject to a 5 percent fee at sale (which is less than 5 percent when applied to domestic equipment) in order to cover proprietary rights on broadcasted material.

Individual Japanese VTR makers are attempting to reinforce their position in the European market for sales of Beta or Video Home System-Type

(VHS) VTRs by arranging for local-based production of videotapes compatible with their product. Sony, for example, has established a plant in Bayonne, France, to produce Beta videotapes, among other items, and Sanyo has countered by granting VHS videotape production technology to the German firm BASF.

RCA has demonstrated its interest in the European home video system market by announcing the development of a European version of its video disc system. The firm has not yet decided whether to license the technology to European firms or invest directly in production. (More basically, though, the question can be raised as to whether RCA will actually follow through on this announcement.)

Asia

The Asian market, excluding China, is a major outlet of consumer electronic products for Japanese firms. In fact, a higher percentage of Japanese television exports in 1978 went to Asian nations than to Western Europe. U.S. firms have virtually no presence in this market. Yet because of the growth of non-Japanese Asian manufacturers, this market area may become less and less lucrative for the Japanese firms.

The Asian market is less uniform than the European market in terms of sophistication and accessibility. Korea, for example, despite the presence of several firms producing color televisions for export, until very recently had no color broadcasting. The Korean market is also heavily protected, with imports subject to 50 percent duty plus 10 percent value-added tax.

In Asia, Taiwan represents the largest consumer electronics export market, with the Republic of Korea a close second. Hong Kong, Singapore, and Malaysia are also sizable export markets.

Latin America

Still in its infancy, the Latin American market possesses significant growth potential. Color broadcasting, limited to a few countries, began about five years ago is only now spreading throughout the region

Japanese manufacturers have been eyeing the area covetously for years and have been developing technical tie-ups and joint ventures. Already five Japanese firms have entered the Brazilian color television market, accompanied by the two major European firms, Telefunken and Philips. Several Japanese firms have plans to enter the newly emerging color television markets in Argentina, Venezuela, and Colombia, among others. The Japanese plan to get established early, allowing them to expand their production in response to growing demand.

Toshiba's careful cultivation of the Central American market is a case in point. In 1971, several years before color broadcasting began, Toshiba entered into a technical cooperation agreement with Inelco of Costa Rica, commissioning the company to make and sell Toshiba-brand products. Five years later, Toshiba set up a local marketing company in Panama in order to broaden its sales network. Now, with its share of the Central American market standing at 45 percent, Toshiba has bought 30 percent of Inelco's shares and added some capital of its own to form a joint venture company, Toshiba Inelco de Costa Rica. The new firm will start making color televisions and other Toshiba-brand products.

Previously Toshiba had formed a joint-venture company, Semp-Toshiba Amazonas S.A., in Brazil, with Semp S.A., one of Brazil's leading consumer electronics manufacturers. Other Japanese firms represented in Brazil are Sharp, Hitachi, Sanyo, and Matsushita. Sharp, the leader in Brazil, is beginning to assemble color televisions in Colombia in 1981 as is Kenia S.A.I.C., an Argentine firm that Sharp supplies with technical assistance.

Other Japanese firms now investing in Latin America include Hitachi, JVC, and Sanyo. Hitachi, which operates black-and-white television plants in Ecuador, Colombia and Costa Rica, has started assembling color sets in Colombia and Costa Rica. JVC has arranged with Jawa Ltda. in Uruguay and Audinac S.A.I.C. in Argentina to assemble its color televisions. Sanyo has formed a joint-venture company in Argentina, which began in May 1980 to produce 2,000 color televisions per month. New Nippon Electric Co. is trying to tie up with local B&W assemblers in Argentina and Venezuela.

Available information indicates that U.S. marketing efforts in Latin America are very limited. Although several U.S. firms operate assembly facilities in Mexico for export to the United States, they market very little locally. Zenith's activity in Latin America is restricted to licensing arrangements in Argentina, Venezuela, and Colombia.

China

The mainland Chinese market potentially could be the biggest and most lucrative in the world. Japanese attempts to establish some type of entry into this market can be taken as a prime example of the aggressive, long-range foreign market strategy of these firms. Matsushita has taken the lead, with plans to build a color television assembly plant capable of turning out 150,000 fourteen-inch sets per year. Matsushita also plans to sell the Chinese a circuit board plant. The most ambitious proposal to date is one by Matsushita to establish a number of fifty-fifty joint ventures between

Japan and China. Although no agreement has been reached, the Matsushita proposal reflects the aggressiveness and flexibility of Japanese firms in devising new-market penetration tactics. In December 1980, Sony signed an agreement with the People's Republic of China to manufacture color television sets in China, paralleling the country's earlier agreement with Matsushita. The People's Republic also has a growing demand for VTRs, which will be used for mass educational programs, and in which Japanese firms will have a substantial market share.

The Chinese have ordered black-and-white picture tube plants from Nippon Electric and Hitachi and have approached TDK about a possible ferrite manufacturing plant for television. They have also been importing finished sets, including 7,000 color televisions from Hitachi in September 1978, and 5,500 black-and-white units per month from Mitsubishi.

Arab States

The Arab market is small but rapidly growing. Japanese firms report increased sales of both color televisions and VTRs to the area, with some indication that the latter is taking over as the new status item. Saudi Arabia, the largest of the Arab markets, imported 8,275 Japanese VTRs in the first five months of 1979, compared with a few dozen the year before. With a wealthy, growing upper stratum of society, the Arab states will continue to offer an important outlet for Japanese products, particularly expensive high-technology ones.

Canada

The Canadian television market was once an American preserve. Westinghouse, Philco-Ford, Fleetwood (later Sylvania), GE, and Admiral all had plants in Canada. But the industry took a turndown in the mid-1970s, in part due to Asian export competition. Both Westinghouse and Philco-Ford had gone under by the time the Canadian government stepped in, imposing special dumping fees on low-priced small-screen color television imports from Japan, Taiwan, and Singapore.

The industry recently has made a comeback, spurred by a production incentive program launched in 1977, and the dumping fees have been discontinued. But in the meantime, the remaining U.S. companies have all gone the way of Westinghouse and Philco-Ford; in their stead are Hitachi, Matsushita, and Sanyo. Moreover Electrohome, Canada's last remaining independent television maker, imports chassis from JVC for all of the televisions it now produces. Canada does, however, remain Zenith's largest export market.

Other Foreign Markets

Few figures are available concerning television supply and demand in other markets, such as Oceania (principally Austrialia and New Zealand) and Africa. Together Oceania and Africa accounted for about 12 percent of Japanese television exports in 1978. Toshiba has formed a joint-venture company in Australia with Rank, its British partner. Both Sony and Hitachi are using their European connections to penetrate the African market—Sony through its tape plant in Bayonne, which exports to French-speaking African countries, and Hitachi through its joint-venture tube company in Finland, which also exports to Africa.

Comparison of U.S. and Japanese
Views on Foreign Markets

A major fault of the U.S. consumer electronics industry, according to many observers, has been its excessive dependence on the home market and its consequent failure to develop foreign markets. Whereas Japanese manufacturers have stressed foreign sales, U.S. producers have been content to sell at home and try to keep the foreigners out. In the process, the U.S. industry has forfeited foreign markets to other producers, primarily the Japanese, and, ironically, paved with way for increased foreign penetration of the U.S. market. The solution to the U.S. industry's ills may be for U.S. firms to develop international market strategies and marketing and distribution systems. In other words, they should emulate the Japanese.

In order to evaluate this proposed solution, let us first review the Japanese experience. Operating in a highly competitive home market, with a strategy of volume production and a concern for the overseas marketability of virtually every new product considered, the Japanese color television industry, aided by the Japanese government, has developed a dynamic export capability. Barred from exporting large-screen color televisions to Europe and facing seemingly entrenched console makers in the United States, the Japanese opted for high-volume production of low-priced portable sets as a means of initial market entry. As they made inroads and profits in the U.S. and European markets, the Japanese plowed these profits back into production of and R&D for more-advanced products, enabling them to move down the learning curve and up the technological ladder. Many Japanese firms moved assembling plants offshore in the 1960s to take advantage of lower labor costs, while the production of advanced componentry was retained in Japan to derive the full benefits of scale. When import barriers against Japanese color televisions began to rise in the mid-1970s along with the yen, Japanese firms switched from exports to investment in foreign markets, especially Europe and the United States. The Japanese also took an early lead in developing the still-uncultivated Latin American and Chinese markets. In sum, the Japanese firms have taken a gradual, long-term approach to foreign markets and are willing to use a wide variety of methods to increase foreign market penetration. One success has led to another for the Japanese, in large part because they have been willing to take risks in penetrating foreign markets and then to reinforce their position by following through on their initial investment.

Significant foreign markets for consumer electronics products exist. Taking advantage of them, however, is quite another story. U.S. producers face two major obstacles. First, just as U.S. and European television makers preempted Japanese firms from entering the large-screen, high-feature end of the market earlier, the Japanese are now in a position to preempt U.S. firms from exploiting the low-priced portable end of the world market, which is vital to sustain any high-volume export drive. Second, U.S. firms seeking to exploit foreign markets by producing locally will have to compete against Japanese firms, many of them now firmly entrenched in those markets.

Finally, one is left with the question of whether U.S. firms have the will to develop international strategies. Despite Japanese inroads into the U.S. market, the two major U.S. manufacturers, Zenith and RCA, still control roughly 40 percent of the market. Why should these increasingly risk-averting U.S. firms venture abroad when the home market remains so substantial and marketing outside is considered difficult and marginal in the short term? One reason is that the longer the U.S. industry fails to take a global approach to its operations, the more it undermines its long-term competitiveness. Zenith and RCA may be able to maintain their U.S. market shares indefinitely, but as the Japanese continue to increase their earnings by exploiting foreign markets, they will surely make even greater inroads in the U.S. market, at the expense of GE and GTE and eventually RCA and Zenith, and develop new, more-sophisticated products and production processes. Token efforts in foreign markets by U.S. firms will not be sufficient in view of current Japanese strength. RCA's intent to develop a European version of its low-cost video disc system shows that it at least recognizes the nature of the challenge; whether RCA can successfully market this product remains to be seen.

Part V
The Japanese Automobile
Industry

10 Competitive Underpinnings of the Industry

In many ways the corporate strategies of Japanese automobile manufacturers parallel those of the Japanese consumer electronics industry. Both industries are committed strongly to long-range management of technological resources; Japanese automobile and consumer electronics firms, for example, expend relatively large amounts of funds annually for R&D and redesigning and reengineering work, which is promoted by a favorable tax environment. Both industries' production strategies call for increasingly automated, high-volume, onshore production; lower per-unit costs and higher-quality products are the twin objectives. Integral to a manufacturing strategy calling for increasing production volumes is an aggressive, imaginative drive for export markets to absorb higher output levels. (Japanese industries have been aided in this in recent years by an undervalued yen, due to the country's high oil bill.) Finally, both industries benefit from their relationships with their respective supplier industries, which are composed in general of responsive, inexpensive subcontractors. The corporate policies that have brought success to the Japanese consumer electronics industry are not restricted to that industry.

Production and Markets

The Japanese automobile industry has now replaced the U.S. industry as the world's leading producer of cars; its output in 1980 was 11,042,844 vehicles. For the past several years the Japanese automobile industry has been intent upon surpassing its U.S. competitors, and growth in Japanese production volumes reflects the determination to achieve this goal. From 1975 to 1979, the Japanese industry enjoyed an average annual production rate of over 8 percent. At a time when U.S. automobile manufacturing facilities are suffering from underutilization, Japan's total automobile production capacity will expand to 12 million units by 1982, a 30 percent jump in capacity from the 1978 level of 9.3 million units.

The Japanese automobile industry is extremely competitive, with nine domestic manufacturers, the smallest producing over 200,000 vehicles annually. Because the domestic vehicle market is close to the saturation point, the Japanese automobile industry was faced with the choice of either aggressively seeking export markets or rationalizing production to a greater degree through mergers or acquisitions, and in fact, several of the smaller automakers are affiliated with the larger manufacturers.

Since 1960, two companies, Toyota and Nissan, have dominated the Japanese industry, accounting today for two-thirds of the production of passenger cars and slightly over one-half of the production of commercial vehicles.

Toyota is Japan's largest vehicle producer and is the third largest automobile firm in the world, behind General Motors and Ford; annual production in 1978 was 2.5 million units. Nissan, the maker of Datsun vehicles, is Japan's second largest automobile firm and the fourth largest in the world, with 2.3 million units manufactured in 1978.

In descending order Japan's other major vehicle manufacturing firms are (1978 world ranking and production figures in parentheses): Toyo Kogyo (eleventh largest, with 717,000 units); Mitsubishi (thirteenth largest, with 648,000 units); Honda (sixteenth largest, with 560,000 units); Isuzu (twenty-fourth largest, with 335,000 units); Daihatsu, which is affiliated with Toyota (twenty-seventh largest, with 261,000 units); Fuji Heavy Industries, which makes Subarus and is affiliated with Nissan (thirty-second largest, with 241,000 units); and Suzuki (thirty-third largest, with 202,000 units). In line with the trend toward a concentration of production in the world automobile industry, Suzuki is expected to be amalgamated into the Toyota group, Mitsubishi is linked with Chrysler, and Isuzu with General Motors.

Individual Japanese firms in general produce a range of vehicles from the minicar to medium-size sedans. Although the domestic market has traditionally favored smaller-sized cars, the Japanese automakers also make their initial inroads into export markets with cars of this size. In an attempt to capture larger shares of export markets, the Japanese auto firms are expanding their product line to include larger vehicles. In West Germany, for example, two Japanese firms offered 12 models in 1975; by 1979 five firms were offering 28 models and 122 variants. (This phenomenon also occurred in the Japanese penetration of the U.S. consumer electronics markets.) Buses and light commercial trucks are also becoming a significant export product for Japanese manufacturers.

The domestic automobile market has been extremely important to the Japanese manufacturers and, like the consumer electronics market, was protected in the developing stages. The industry as a whole exports about 48 percent of its output, as compared with the export of 52 percent of the output of the French and West German industries. Japan is the second largest automobile market in the world, representing over 8 percent of this market, behind the United States, which accounts for just over 40 percent. At present, there is approximately one car for every four people in Japan, as compared to approximately one car for every two people in the United States.

Yet while the domestic market remains an important commercial battleground for the Japanese automakers, especially for the replacement market, it is becoming increasingly apparent that the long-term success of individual Japanese auto manufacturers hinges on their continued ability to expand into export markets. The Japanese market is expected to stabilize in the early 1980s due to sheer geographic absorption, thus making export markets the principal outlet for expanding production volumes.

Since 1974 Japan has been the world's largest exporter of automobiles. By 1979 the Japanese industry was exporting over 4.5 million units (as compared to 2.6 million in 1974), far outpacing France, its nearest international competitor, which exported 2.4 million units in 1979. Japanese exports have been rising steadily over the past few years, and the industry continues to announce expansion plans. Given the inability of the domestic market to absorb the projected production increase, there is a compulsive necessity to continue to expand exports. With roughly 40 percent going to the United States, this represents the largest single export market for Japanese firms.

Although the Japanese industry is aggressively attempting to expand its share of the U.S. market (over 20 percent in 1979), it is also conducting intensive marketing campaigns throughout the rest of the world. More than any other national automobile industry, the Japanese industry's export activities span the globe. In the ten years from 1969 to 1979, Japanese automobile exports increased by over 480 percent. To put this in perspective, exports in 1977 to the United States totaled 1.7 million vehicles; they increased 76 percent by 1979, totaling over 3 million units. In 1977, exports to Europe came to 760,000; Southeast Asia, 470,000; Middle East, 437,000; Oceania, 296,000; Central and South America, 273,000; and Africa, 262,000.

On the other hand, automobile imports into Japan remain minimal, a result of both the strong hold maintained on the market by Japanese firms and other nontariff barriers (including a complex distribution system), which have made the market all but impenetrable in the past to foreign firms. Also imports into Japan frequently fail to measure up to quality expectations or demands of Japanese consumers; certain specifications are often lacking. No U.S. auto manufacturer, for example, produces right-hand drive cars, and Japan, like England, is a right-hand drive country. As another example, Japanese consumers generally feel that the paint job on U.S. autos is inferior to that of Japanese cars. Imports for the past several years have never exceeded 2 percent of national new-car registrations. In 1979 approximately 17,000 U.S.-made automobiles were sold in Japan, as compared to the 2 million Japanese vehicles sold in the United States that year, and total Japanese imports of foreign cars in that year were just over 60,000 units.

Historical Development and Government Involvement

The Japanese automobile industry was insignificant up to the late 1930s and did not become international in scope until the 1970s. The shape and directions the industry has taken in more recent times are influenced by a number of historical forces: the threat of foreign competition, the role of the government, and the national trade balance.

In the 1930s Ford and General Motors controlled 85 percent of the Japanese passenger car market, producing over 30,000 units annually from parts and subassemblies imported from the United States. The domestic industry achieved very little growth, composed as it was of very small firms operating with inferior scale, technology, and capital resources; annual production did not exceed 500 units before 1930. That automobile production fell to the strictly private, small-capital sector was due in large part to an absence of Japanese government interest in fostering a domestic industry. In the government's view, automobile production was a highly speculative enterprise and of lower priority to the national interest than steel, coal, and other heavy industry. This view was shared by the powerful and diversified *zaibatsu* groups of Mitsubishi, Misui, and Sumitomo, each one of which separately considered and rejected entry into the automotive business. (The *zaibatsu* organization was a very large holding company, which was generally controlled by a wealthy family clan. An individual *zaibatsu* formed a collection of manufacturing, trading, and financial corporations. A handful of these *zaibatsus* were a dominant force in the pre-World War II Japanese economy. Some of the present-day large corporations trace their lineage to the pre-World War II *zaibatsu* period, but in contrast to the prewar groups, they are loosely linked to associated business groups, both legally and managerially.) Because of this, a large number of small manufacturers were able to gain a significant portion of the growing automotive market in Japan.

During the 1930s the government's attitude toward an automobile industry changed, in part out of a recognition that its military ambitions in Asia required production of heavy vehicles. In addition, then-current long-range economic considerations pointed toward the need to articulate some form of national automobile development policy. While still harboring strong doubts as to the economic wisdom of fostering a domestic industry, the Japanese government nevertheless was becoming increasingly aware that if onshore foreign capital was permitted unlimited production levels, it would continue to dominate the domestic market and hence preclude development of Japanese producers. The high failure rate of small domestic producers and the continued unwillingness of the *zaibatsus* to compete, even at the later invitation by the government, convinced economic planners that protection from foreign capital was essential for the development of domestic industry.

Another dimension in the government's reconsideration of an automobile industry was Japan's foreign exchange situation, whose precariousness was dramatically underlined by the international monetary crises and trade dislocations of the late 1920s and early 1930s. The lack of a domestic automobile industry placed strong demands on the country's foreign-exchange reserves to pay for imported finished vehicles or parts for assembly. Domestic automobile assembly and parts manufacture would reduce net imports and provide much-needed industrial employment and income.

This awareness was translated into policy in 1936 with enactment of the Automobile Manufacturing Enterprise Law, designed principally to curtail the activity of foreign producers onshore and to stimulate domestic producers. The law imposed annual production ceilings on foreign producers, and the tariff rates on imported parts were raised. In 1937 a provisional law eliminated imports of strategic commodities. Soon thereafter the combined laws had their desired effect; Ford's and General Motors' penetration decreased dramatically.

To Japanese producers, the law extended a variety of generous benefits, including exemption from income tax for five years, a five-year rebate on import customs duty, and a relaxation in the legal requirements for recapitalization. By 1937 Nissan and Toyota, along with the truck manufacturer Isuzu, dominated automobile production in Japan with a combined 80 percent share of the national market. A negligible number of passenger cars were made in the prewar period, with buses and trucks (one-half of which were consumed by the military) constituting the major portion of production. The year 1938 marked both the peak year for passenger car output (2,000 units) and the point at which automakers turned increasingly to military vehicle production.

The question of whether Japan should have its own automotive industry was again debated within the government for several years after the war. The newly formed MITI argued for redevelopment of the industry, with an emphasis on passenger car production, based on foreign technology and government financial assistance. The opposing point of view, represented by the Bank of Japan, asserted that the scarcity of capital and immense reconstruction task ahead dictated that Japan concentrate resources into areas of comparative advantage, which did not include automobile production. Both sides realized, though, that demand, at least in the short run, would be met through imports; the reentry of foreign capital, however, was never considered as an alternative.

Although these opposing viewpoints were based on different principles—the former sought infant industry protection, while the latter was based on the theory of comparative advantage—they both shared the recognition that the Japanese automobile industry at the time was far behind those of the industrially advanced nations. The scarcity of automobiles in

Japan and the expectation that the foreign-exchange constraints would continue gave considerable weight to the arguments advanced by MITI and its supporters. The matter was finally settled by the Korean War, since the automotive needs of the United Nations forces created a timely growth opportunity for Japanese producers. The automobile industry was thus placed under strong government protection as one of the economy's strategic industries, along with synthetic fibers, petrochemicals, and electronics.

Government protection for the industry consisted of quotas, tariffs, and commodity taxes. Although a quota system for automobile imports had been in effect since the end of World War II, by the early 1950s its chief function had changed from the original one of conserving scarce foreign exchange to protecting the infant domestic automobile producers from foreign competition. Japan's tariff rate structure was both high overall and designed to favor domestic producers. For example, tariff rates were much higher on smaller passenger cars than on trucks and larger cars, where Japanese producers were either fully competitive or not competing at all. In addition, the commodity tax structure discriminated predominantly against foreign, large cars in an effort to shift demand to Japanese models. Having removed quotas in 1965 and eliminating soon thereafter most of the tariffs and commodity relief enjoyed by domestic manufacturers, the government today retains little of this protectionist machinery.

Recognizing the strategic role it could play in the economy as a whole, the Japanese government in 1951 also took special steps to provide the automobile industry with the necessary capital for expansion and modernization through special tax arrangements and subsidies. Later the auto parts industry was included under these same provisions. On MITI's recommendation, the Japan Development Bank extended a series of reconstruction loans to the auto producers during the period 1951 to 1955. The value of these transactions to the industry far exceeded the monetary value of the loans (which were of nominal amounts) in that they served as a demonstration of the government's support of the industry and thereby encouraged commercial banks to extend credit as well.

It soon became evident to both the economic planners and the companies themselves that no amount of protection and financial support could compensate for the low technical level of the Japanese auto manufacturing capabilities. There was a consensus that foreign technology needed to be obtained, and MITI selectively began to approve applications from the auto companies to assemble knock-down imported components from foreign, primarily European, manufacturers. In 1952-1953, four domestic firms negotiated individual five- to seven-year contracts: Nissan with Austin of the United Kingdom to assemble 1,200 units a year; Isuzu with Hillman, also of the United Kingdom, to assemble 1,200 units annually; Hino with Renault to assemble 1,300 of the French vehicles annually; and Mitsubishi with Willy's Jeep.

Nissan was the only company of the four with previous experience in passenger car production. In fact, it was largely the decision to license technology from abroad that permitted existing truck manufacturers in Japan to enter passenger car production. Toyota and Prince, however, depended exclusively on domestic expertise, and the four licensees were soon in a position to upgrade their own technology. The assembly of European knockdown cars lasted a relatively short time, and by 1958 nearly every passenger car assembled in Japan was of domestic design and manufacture.

The years 1960 to 1975 constituted a unique period for the Japanese economy as a whole and for the automobile industry in particular. During this period of rapid expansion and growth, Japan evolved into a major world economic power. The Japanese automakers were encouraged by and responded to the growing domestic automobile market. Their primary objective, at least initially, was to secure a position in the Japanese market, which in turn would support the necessary scale of operation essential to their establishment as viable firms. All of the manufacturers shared the objective of upgrading the technical quality of the product, while continuing growth in sales and achieving unit-cost reductions through expanded capacity and improved efficiency. Only later in the period was expansion of export markets an important concern of the automobile manufacturers.

A mass market for passenger cars was quickly becoming a reality after 1965, in large part due to persistent guidance and regulation by the Japanese government. The government's involvement included the design of a tax structure that favored smaller-sized cars, an increase in highway construction budgets, and strict enforcement of biennial automobile inspection. The last measure had the effect of encouraging car owners to purchase a new car every four years because each inspection cost an owner as much as $300 to bring a car's performance up to standard.

Despite the fact that the government never succeeded in its principal objective of significantly reducing the number of producers in the industry, it made several essential contributions to the industry's development through the late 1960s. MITI first recognized the strategic role that an automobile industry could play in Japan's postwar economy and defended the industry's position against the opposing strategy of the Bank of Japan. It instituted the protectionist measures necessary for the infant industry's development and admitted into the country unassembled foreign cars in order to build a domestic technological base in automotive production. The timely extension of low-cost capital by the government played an important role in the strengthening of the industry. Finally, the government helped in developing the domestic market. Many of these government policies are similar to those directed toward the consumer electronics industry.

The government was instrumental in getting the industry started and in nurturing its development. It did not dominate or monopolize the producers, however. The initiative for development originated with the companies, and technological and economic success depended on their individual efforts alone. By 1960 the present-day competitive structure of the automobile industry in Japan had already emerged. As the Japanese automobile industry grew increasingly internationally competitive in the 1960s and 1970s, it also grew less receptive to government involvement in the industry. Thus as with the consumer electronics firms, the Japanese automobile firms have been concerned primarily with their own corporate interests and consider as secondary those interests that the Japanese government deems beneficial for the nation as a whole. Nevertheless the country as a whole has benefited from this situation in that the pursuit by the Japanese government and industry of their respective interests frequently have been mutually reinforcing. In the aftermath of the 1973 oil crisis, for example, the Japanese government was extremely concerned with foreign-exchange generation and reduction of oil imports at a time when Japanese automakers were gearing up for their intensive sustained assault on export markets and developing more-fuel-efficient automobiles.

Corporate Strategies

As with the consumer electronics industry, the central corporate strategy guiding the Japanese automobile industry is based on a commitment to expand production volumes. From this commitment flow several other strategies that also greatly enhance the Japanese industry's international competitiveness. Company policies for increasing R&D and production upgrading through redesigning, reengineering, and automation have an intrinsic value, and their benefits are compounded when coupled with expansion of production volumes in an industry where scale economies are critical for success. Additionally the respect that Japanese firms have earned as expert international marketing organizations stems from their need to secure export markets for increased production volumes. Finally, the Japanese automobile industry (like the consumer electronics industry) has developed a form of vertical integration both internally and with its supply industries that is highly responsive to the exigencies of production volume expansions.

Volume Production and the Technology Factor

The cardinal principle of the Japanese automobile industry has been to increase volume as rapidly as possible as a means of decreasing unit costs. Additionally the Japanese, in contrast to most American companies, consistently apply the so-called learning-curve management principle. Most U.S. firms therefore operate on a much flatter curve than do the Japanese with regard to rate of increase of output and derived efficiencies from learning and unit-cost decreases. As a result, the manufacturing costs of Nissan, Toyota, and Honda, for example, are estimated as being 40 to 50 percent lower than those of European or American firms.

Individual automakers have adopted various means for achieving scale economies while preserving the appearances of specialization and customizing. Nissan's triplet car system seeks thorough production rationalization using common auto parts and common production facilities to a degree unmatched by U.S. competitors. "Triplets" refers to three new model changes introduced to the market by Nissan between May and August 1977. These three car models are equipped with the same engines and chassis, and their bodies are designed along the same basic lines. A large number of common parts are installed in the three models, yet the use of different exterior parts, such as front grills or bumpers, on each model gives them a different appearance.

Efforts to achieve economies of scale are also evident in production processes adopted by the Japanese automakers. One process that has been instituted in many plants is the simultaneous production of different model cars. The assembly line, consisting of as many lines as there are models being produced, is provided with necessary parts in conformity with the moving speed and direction of the lines, through computer operations. The timing of the supply and application of the parts to bodies is organized by the computer. While various kinds of cars are assembled simultaneously, the same parts are often applied to different model cars.

The Japanese automobile industry's ability to design and engineer industrial products and production systems and effectively manage them at successive stages of market growth has been essential to its successful production strategy. As wages have risen (they are still lower than comparable wages in the United States or Europe), Japan has maintained its competitiveness in world markets through continuing rationalization and modernization of its industrial plants and production methods, progressively improving its cost-effectiveness through constant value engineering of components and parts and improvement of overall product design. Of all Japanese industries, these capabilities have perhaps best been demonstrated by the automobile industry.

Japanese automobile companies have made remarkable achievements in designing and engineering production processes to improve production rationalization. Mitsubishi's plant in Okazaki, built in 1978, illustrates these efforts. The plant, which produces two different passenger car models, was structured with a view toward increasing automation, rationalization, quality improvement, and resources and energy savings. According to Mitsubishi, the plant has forty-seven robotized units (produced by Mitsubishi Heavy Industries) for the welding of car bodies and eight automatic painting machines; the plant is 75 percent automated and employs only 1,250 workers. The plant layout is designed to rationalize material flow from the press line right through the assembly line. Furthermore it is equipped with ten computers for easy model changeover and additions and for speedy and accurate inspection checkup.

The key to the Japanese automobile firms' generally successful efforts to increase production volumes through technological upgrading has lain in their willingness to make the necessary capital expenditures. Toyota alone has a $2 billion reserve fund for the upgrading of production technology. Nissan currently is investing $229 million in construction work alone for a new product line and technical development center. A simple ratio illustrates how much more committed the Japanese automobile firms are to make the requisite capital outlays for advanced production processes: in 1968, Toyota's plants housed about $16,000 worth of equipment for each plant employee, while General Motor's plants averaged $11,900 in equipment per plant employee; by 1978, it has been estimated that Toyota's ratio more than doubled to $50,800 in equipment per worker, while General Motors's 1978 ratio actually decreased a bit from the 1968 level.

The U.S. automobile industry recently has made a substantial effort to make the necessary capital commitment to reengineer automotive products, but only after foreign (mostly Japanese) imports had captured over 21 percent of the U.S. market. Chrysler in particular, and to a lesser extent Ford, are indicative of reactions that were too long delayed and responses that may still be inadequate in stemming the growing tide of Japanese imports. The movement of production facilities for major components to Mexico and Brazil is reminiscent of the U.S. consumer electronics industry's efforts to achieve cost reductions by moving to low-wage countries rather than by automating and robotizing facilities to meet the foreign competition. (Part of the reason for establishing production for export in Mexico and Brazil undoubtedly has been pressures of the governments in these countries to do so or face low market shares. But the adverse effects on U.S.-based technological parities have nonetheless followed.)

The Chrysler situation is symptomatic of the difficulties that U.S. industry in general is having in technological adjustment to economic change. A similar situation arose in the case of Toyo Kogyo, Japan's third largest automobile manufacturer, producing the Mazda car. After the 1973 oil embargo and soaring gasoline prices, Mazda sales declined rapidly. Although the car was powered by the innovative rotary engine, it was also relatively fuel inefficient. By 1975 the company faced bankruptcy, which would have put 100,000 Toyo Kogyo employees out of work, as well as countless suppliers. At this stage, the Japanese government did nothing more than encourage private-sector rescue attempts; the Japanese banking community serves as the protector of Japanese industry much more than does the government. In this case, Toyo Kogyo's main bank, Sumitomo, took the initiative in making the auto firm more competitive. Aside from making some shifts in management, slashing dividends, and reducing the work force by offering early retirement bonuses, Sumitomo helped raise a $1 billion syndicated loan. The money was targeted for plant modernization and redesigning and reengineering the Mazda. Within two years, Toyo Kogyo had put a fuel-efficient subcompact in the Japanese and U.S. markets, which sold briskly. By 1978 the company perfected a fuel-efficient rotary engine, and sales of its rotary engine sport coupe took off dramatically. In 1979, a healthy Toyo Kogyo realized a record profit of $30 million, despite the loan repayment burden to Sumitomo.[1]

In regard to the Chrysler situation, two facets of Toyo Kogyo's recovery stand out. First, the Japanese government may provide strong protection for an infant industry, but once several companies in the industry have established themselves in the domestic market, intense competition is the rule. Uncompetitive firms are not assisted by the government, which is more concerned with the overall international competition of the industry rather than the domestic competitiveness of individual firms. Second, Toyo Kogyo realized, as all other Japanese firms do, that it could not rely on a government bailout but had to take the necessary long-range steps, including capital outlays, to regain its competitiveness. The upgrading of product and process technology was regarded as the key to a restoration of the firm's health.

The corporate structure of several Japanese automakers has also contributed to the continued strengthening of their manufacturing operations. In these firms the manufacturing, designing, and engineering functions are kept separate from the marketing, sales, and distribution functions by means of separate companies responsible for these two sets of functions. Toyota Motor Company, for example, is engaged in designing, engineering, and producing automobiles, which Toyota Sales Company then markets; the latter determines market needs, changes, and size, and the former translates these data into actual products. Outside of this information exchange between the manufacturing and marketing groups, involvement by one group in the operations of the other is kept to a minimum, thus allowing each to pursue its functions more efficiently. In contrast, U.S. auto firms' marketing and production operations are much more closely linked, to the point that they disrupt each other's activities.

Export Strategy

In order to achieve and maintain their high production volumes, Japanese automakers must look beyond the domestic market to absorb their output. In contrast to U.S. automobile firms, the Japanese industry does not place great weight on projections of world demand in establishing production capacity targets; Japanese automakers add capacity first and then search for overseas markets to absorb what the domestic market cannot. In fact, it has only been the existence of export markets that has permitted some of the late entrants, such as Honda, to achieve sufficient economies of scale in automobile production. (Honda exports 75 percent of its output.) Due to the difficulties of increasing penetration of the domestic market, Honda was forced to cultivate export markets if it was to achieve an efficient scale of production. In recent years export markets have also served to sustain the economies of scale built into Japanese automobile production when domestic demand has become stagnant. It is this phenomenon that underlies the observation that Japanese exports are stepped up at times of recession and are constricted during economic recovery or abnormally high-growth periods. Highly competitive pricing of exports also accompanies slow domestic growth periods.

Several principles that have guided the Japanese consumer electronics industry in its efforts to increase export are also found in the nation's auto industry. Established foreign markets, such as the United States, were entered through gaps at the bottom of the market (in this case smaller, cheaper cars). Although Japanese automobiles in foreign markets may initially enjoy price advantages (not infrequently due to foreign exchange rate levels), and this is critical in establishing market penetration, the Japanese manufacturers gradually shift marketing emphasis to quality, performance, and service as a means of broadening market appeal. The Japanese automobile (and consumer electronics) firms also have invested heavily in consumer and market research in foreign markets in order to identify opportunity areas. And these firms have been assisted in this and distributing activities by the far-flung networks of Japanese trading companies.

Japanese automakers generally avoid or delay to the maximum other countries' protectionist measures arising from high levels of Japanese auto imports. The Japanese industry will produce offshore for a foreign market as a last resort—for example, if protectionist actions threaten to close a given export market. Japanese automobile manufacturing facilities in other countries have been characterized by low-technology operations; advanced automation and production of high-technology components are retained at home.

The success of Japanese cars and light trucks in U.S. and Western European markets has resulted in restrictions of Japanese imports, and other protectionist reactions are imminent. Japanese firms have reacted with plans to invest in production facilities to continue to maintain their position in these markets, just as they did in the case of color television receivers. Nissan is now assemblying trucks in Tennessee, and Honda has started an assembly operation in the United States. Nissan is negotiating a joint venture in the United Kingdom, which it intends to use as a major entry point to the European Community market. Nissan also now has joint ventures in Italy (with Alpha Romeo) and in Spain (with Motor Iberica) and are negotiating a major joint venture with Volkswagen in Germany. Volkswagen and Nissan are working on a reciprocal arrangement under which Nissan will assemble and partially manufacture VWs in Japan for the Japanese markets and Volkswagen will assemble and partially manufacture Nissan products in its U.S. plant for the U.S. market.

Vertical Intergration and
Supplier Industries

One of the most salient characteristics of the Japanese automobile industry is its high degree of vertical integration. Automobile companies in Japan have strived toward self-sufficiency in the forward and backward linkages of production due to two important features of the industry. First, the high fixed costs in plant and equipment needed for automobile manufacture dictate that economies of scale are extremely important at every stage of operation. Second, in Japan during the 1930s and 1940s, firms in several industries recognized that the inadequacies of Japan's basic industries could be overcome only by producing basic materials and major components internally. For example, the Aichi Steel Works, Ltd., has its origins in the steel works department that was established in 1935 by the Toyoda Automatic Loom Works. In 1940 that department was separated and made an independent company called the Toyoda Steel Works, Ltd., the direct predecessor of Aichi Steel Works. The role of both Toyoda and Aichi Steel Works has been to keep Toyota adequately supplied with special steels, a vital basic material, recognized as holding the key to mass production.

The extent of vertical integration in Japanese industry must be viewed in relation to supplier industries. The benefits of vertical integration in Japan are derived in great part through unconventional structural patterns or relationships with supplier industries, illustrated by Toyota Motor Company's production system. The low level of internal parts production done by Toyota itself is strongly supplemented by a tight supplier-purchaser relationship. The Toyota Motor group embraces companies in different industries. Essentially controlled by the Toyoda family, the group is roughly divided into two major subgroups. The first subgroup is composed of twelve corporations closely related to the Toyoda family. The second subgroup comprises other companies linked with the group through business transactions.

The twelve companies belonging in the first subgroup are directly controlled by the Toyota Motor Company. A variety of industries are represented in this group, such as specialty steel, textiles, machine tools, and trading (in nonautomobile products). Belonging to the second subgroup are mostly local companies operating in the Tokai region surrounding Nagoya and closely connected with the automobile operations of Toyota. Toyota directly or indirectly provides these firms with funds and production processes. The companies principally serve as Toyota's suppliers. Toyota relies on over 280 subcontractors, who in turn rely on an even larger number of smaller firms; in all, Toyota may use the services of over 25,000 Japanese firms.

In a number of these companies, Toyota exercises control through stock ownership, which usually amounts to a 20 to 30 percent equity position. It is often through these subsidiary relationships that the company achieves the kind of vertical intergration typical of large American and European automakers. In general, Nissan's production system and parts procurement practices are quite similar to those of Toyota, except that it typically maintains tighter control, owning as much as 50 percent of the parts companies' stock. Even in the absence of stock ownership, there exists within the Japanese enterprise system a keen awareness of the strong interdependencies among the different companies developed through historical, family, or structural ties.

The vertically integrated relationship Japanese automakers maintain with parts suppliers has greatly facilitated efforts to expand capacity or increase efficiency to reduce costs or improve technical quality of products or production methods. The *Kanban* (on-time delivery) system, which is used by several Japanese automakers, is a case in point. In this system supplier firms deliver shipments of parts and components to automakers' production plants virtually hours before they will go on the assembly line. In this way much less investment for parts inventory is needed by the automobile firms, and thus operating costs are reduced. Additionally changes in parts specifications by automakers do not cause the obsolescence of a big inventory of parts. In cases where there is an equity interest, the automaker can exert direct influence on a parts suppliers' operations by placing employees in key management positions and by working with the affiliate's technical personnel. Additional control can be achieved through the placement of a principal stockholder on the board of the supplier enterprise.

Summary

The Japanese challenge to the U.S. automobile industry is similar in several respects to that which overwhelmed U.S. consumer electronics. The intense competition fostered by the domestic auto market has served as a springboard for exporting efforts now central to the Japanese industry's stability and success. Although the government nurtured the early automobile manufacturers, it could not substantially influence the industry's structure. As the industry gained strength, the government found itself at odds with the leading firms and ultimately withdrew from direct involvement. Through expanded production volumes and product lines, technological upgrading, and extensive vertical integration with supplier firms, the major Japanese automakers have created the basis of an export strength that threatens the independent existence of their U.S. counterparts.

Note

1. See Yoshi Tsurumi, "How to Handle the Next Chrysler," *Fortune,* June 16, 1980, pp. 87-88.

11 Epilogue: U.S. Policy Implications

An implicit question throughout this book has been what the United States can learn from the Japanese experience. The answers to this question relate closely to the ongoing national debate concerning innovation and productivity in the U.S. economy. In this context, what we draw from the Japanese experience depends upon our understanding of the major causes of lagging innovation in our economy and declining advances in productivity.

The stakes in an accurate diagnosis are very high. Our political and strategic position in the world depends ultimately upon our economic strength. As a nation, we are like a patient with an incipient heart condition, and we may have to change our life-style if we are to survive. It will not help to blame our situation on conspiracy theories of unfair trade practices and to ignore the real underlying causes of lagging innovational thrust in our economy.

Part of the problem in prescribing corrective action is that our society is based upon a multiplicity of purpose and initiatives, where it is extremely difficult to obtain consensus leading to effective management. The prevailing adversary relationship between government and industry is but one dimension of this problem. As a society, we respond to crisis by mobilizing public will to make the necessary decisions and then take the required action. Like the patient with the incipient heart condition, the best thing that could happen would be a heart attack severe enough to alarm us but benign enough to allow for recovery. Current levels of inflation, unemployment, and industrial decline, such as the Chrysler situation, have not yet forced us to recognize the danger.

A considerable segment of U.S. industry has blamed external forces for much of its difficulties: the meteoric rise of petroleum prices, which have distorted demand for automobile products; inflation and taxation, which have undermined investment incentives; and government regulation which has stifled industry and sapped its efficiency (including antitrust, environmental protection, safety, and fuel economy requirements in automobiles). Others have argued that the basic fault lies with U.S. industrial management, which has undergone profound changes in its composition, philosophy, and practice over the past generation. Some believe that American management is now dominated by financial and legal mentalities that are more concerned with rapid and risk-free returns through small incremental change of existing products or through merger and acquisition rather than through long-term technological development.[1]

The Canon Company's recent efforts to recoup its market position is a good example of Japanese industry's voracious appetite for new markets, which when combined with aggressive world marketing has been so successful in reaching into new product areas. The determination and the ability to redesign and reengineer new product lines has accounted for its formidable success in the U.S. and other world markets. A company like Canon with considerable capabilities in both the electronic and optical fields has made new inroads in camera and office copier fields. Like many other Japanese firms, Canon designs and builds its own fabricating equipment and where necessary has been aggressive in acquiring U.S. companies for essential pieces of new manufacturing technology (mask aligners used in manufacturing the new microprocessors for their equipment). Canon combines its engineering capabilities with the latest marketing techniques, including massive television advertising campaigns, to ensure adequate market penetration.[2]

A related analysis concludes that American firms have failed to keep pace with a highly unstable and unpredictable world.[3] Many of the complaints about an adverse economic environment are a reflection of the new complexities of doing business in today's world economy. In the case of consumer electronics, rather than facing up to these adversities, U.S. firms have chosen the path of least resistance, by moving offshore to low-wage countries, limiting research and development to small, incremental adjustments in the existing product lines, and diversifying into lower-risk, quicker-return commercial activities.

In sharp contrast, Japanese management has been nurtured on the intense competition within the Japanese economy and formidable American and European commercial competition, particularly when they first entered world markets on a significant scale in the 1960s. The Japanese economy is much more vulnerable to destabilizing factors than is the U.S. economy. Many of the economically advantageous traits found in Japan may well derive from the challenge of adversity, a term used by the British historian Arnold Toynbee to help explain the rise and fall of successive civilizations. Included among these traits are the work ethic of its labor force, the dedication of its management to economic survival, and the consumer's propensity to save (which feeds investment in growth industries).

Part of our difficulties in the United States may lie in inhibiting factors in our economic environment. In this regard, the financial and tax structures in the Japanese economy, which favor risk taking and encourage the dynamic pace of innovation, are surely instructive.[4] But a more important lesson can be drawn from the philosophy and practice of Japanese management. The Japanese experience provides invaluable insights on how to manage in the face of adversity and how to remain competitive in a rapidly changing world economy. Indeed the Japanese experience seems to demonstrate that the ability to manage technological change in a dynamic world economy may well be the decisive competitive advantage in world trade.

Two other distinctive changes in our economic environment dictate that we change our economic life-style. One is our growing level of international trade as a percentage of our gross national product (approaching 10 percent). The other is acute shortages on a global scale in capital, energy and other raw material resources, and even technology (as in the automation and robotics field), all of which have contributed to the loss of competitiveness in particular areas. For the first time in peacetime history, the U.S. economy has had to learn to grapple with the problem of such shortages and, thus, global interdependency. Once again the Japanese experience has much to teach us on how to cope more effectively with a condition with which that country has had to contend for decades.

A fundamental U.S. economic policy issue is the extent to which we will continue to rely on market mechanisms and a free trade system for improvements in our economic performance and in the lagging levels of productivity and innovation. The tendencies in both the consumer electronics and automobile industries have been toward protectionism and other forms of government intervention to assist ailing industries, as in the Chrysler case. There is also the question of the extent to which the U.S. government can and should intervene in support of innovational dynamics (at least to the extent of modifying existing laws and regulations that inhibit them).[5] The danger is that if we continue to rely on market mechanisms and do nothing to prevent further inroads into our markets by Japanese industry or to improve the innovational thrust in our own industries, U.S.-based production will continue to deteriorate and decline.

In both the consumer electronics and automobile industry U.S. management was not as responsive to incipient shifts in consumer preferences as was its Japanese competitors. Another basic shortcoming of American management has been its preoccupation with U.S. markets and U.S. competition, ignoring the potential threat to U.S. markets from foreign manufacturers as astute and determined as the Japanese turned out to be. In short, American firms paid lip-service to market forces when in fact they were largely ignoring them, and as a result many have suffered near-catastrophic setbacks. The irony is that the market mechanisms that both consumers and producers have come to depend upon for efficiency and appropriate signals have failed us by default.

Clearly we need to improve the U.S. economic environment affecting innovation and industrial management's response to the Japanese competitive challenge. This may require in part that corporate tax incentives be more definitively linked to investments in the technological upgrading of U.S.-based industry, in the related retraining of industrial labor, and in other activities leading to an expansion of U.S. industrial exports. Adjustments in these areas will have to be sufficient to offset the very considerable comparative advantage that Japan now has in the quality of its work force and in a social organization highly supportive of industrial efficiency and responsive to rapid changes in the world economy. Japanese advantage in the area of social organization includes the ability of government and industry to work closely together in anticipating technological change, in jointly planning necessary or advantageous adjustments, and in obtaining the consensus and support of involved financial and labor communities. In this sense, Japan Inc. is indeed a reality; there is not a government-management conspiracy but a commitment by the Japanese people at all levels of the economic system to make one's company, and by extension one's country, a world leader. The Japanese talent for consensus and the productive harmonization of competing interests has deep sociocultural foundations in the historical structure of the nation's family-based, diversified trading and manufacturing companies. In our own case, a reevaluation of antitrust regulations and other factors fostering inefficient, self-defeating adversary relationships in American industry is clearly necessary.

Another major problem with U.S. management is that the effect of economic conditions on technological development is overlooked or simply ignored. For example, the depreciation of the dollar against the yen (raising the export price of Japanese goods to U.S. markets) has put pressure on Japanese industry to improve further productivity and product design competitiveness so as not to price itself out of the U.S. market. Conversely devaluation has meant that U.S. domestic prices relative to imports are reduced, which in turn takes the pressure off U.S. manufacturing to improve its products and productivity to compete with foreign products. The combined effects may well have contributed to U.S. industry's lapsing into progressive technological disadvantage relative to Japan.

It should also be evident that Japanese investments in U.S. assembly facilities are not a solution to the problem of maintaining U.S. industrial employment in the long run. In fact, these plants permit Japanese firms to continue to design and produce sophisticated componentry in Japan and thereby reinforce their technological lead through access to, and earnings from, the U.S. market. Similarly the relocation of production by U.S. firms to low-wage, offshore sites in effect avoids the problem of technical adjustment to economic change.

A related issue concerns U.S. pressure on the Japanese authorities to increase their military expenditures. The U.S. government has been urging the

Japanese government to double the level of its military expenditures from the approximately 1 to 2 percent level to 9 to 10 percent of the gross national product. This policy may have adverse side effects on the widening technology and management gap between the two countries. Such expansion inevitably would involve technology sharing under coproduction agreements covering the manufacture of military air and ground equipment, areas where U.S. industry still has a substantial technical lead, particularly in supersonic aircraft, space communications, microprocessors, and advanced computer applications. Japanese industrial firms have demonstrated capabilities to adapt, redesign, and reengineer acquired prototypes in response to commercial market opportunities. Military production agreements of this kind could easily afford additional channels for technological erosion of other U.S. industrial segments at a time when our economy is already seriously threatened in this regard.

By way of summary, two points warrant emphasis. One concerns the general problem of technological adjustments in a changing world economy and the necessity of maintaining the innovational thrust in our industry rather than becoming preoccupied with salvaging moribund companies (the Chrysler syndrome). The other relates to multiplicity of purpose and initiative (including market mechanisms and the free trade system), which served us so well in the past but now has deteriorated to debilitating confrontation or impasse in several segments of our industrial economy. The fundamental challenge in managing our economy is to find effective means for achieving national consensus on some of the vital adjustment issues that we now face. We must find ways and means to determine what has gone wrong and then decide what action is to be taken in terms of involved constituencies of government, industry, labor, and finance.

Notes

1. See Robert H. Hayes and William T. Abernathy, "Managing Our Way to Economic Decline," *Harvard Business Review* (July-August 1980). The authors point out that in the automobile industry U.S. management has sacrificed product-design flexibility for short-run production efficiencies and has overrelied on equipment suppliers for process innovation.

2. See Louis Kraar, "Japan's Canon Focuses on America," *Fortune,* January 12, 1981, pp. 82ff.

3. See Peter F. Drucker, *Managing in Turbulent Times* (New York: Harper and Row, 1980.)

4. See also Jack Baranson's testimony and recommendation to Joint Hearings on Export Policy before the Subcommittee on International Finance and Subcommittee on Science, Technology, and Space, 95th Cong., 2d sess., May 16, 1978, pp. 27-36.

5. See, for example, National Academy of Engineering, *Industrial Innovation and Public Policy Options: Report to Colloquium* (Washington, D.C., 1980).

Appendix A: Technological Innovations in the Television Industry

The picture tube is one of the major parts of a color television set. In Japan, the initial technology to produce the picture tube was acquired from RCA. The red fluorescent material used in early color picture tubes was of much lower efficiency than that used in black-and-white television, and hence the luminous intensity was rather low. Sylvania succeeded in developing a fluorescent material using rare earth elements, which resulted in enhancing luminous intensity by as much as 50 percent. One reason why color television was not popular at first was that the quality did not match the high price. This improvement on the fluorescent material was a big step toward full-scale popularization of color television.

The next important improvement on technology was the picture tube using the black matrix method. First developed by Zenith in the United States, this innovation achieved a much better contrast between areas of fluorescent dots on black material such as carbon. In Japan, this process was improved and developed into the stripe method in 1971 with fluorescent bodies arranged in vertical stripes. The advent of the black matrix method brought the picture quality of color picture tubes nearly to the level of black-and-white television. The other important development in picture tube technology was Sony's Trinitron tube in 1969.

Other significant developments in color picture tubes have been made by widening the deflection angle and by improving the electronic gun. The 70-degree deflection tube became 90 degree deflection in 1963, and 110 degree in 1971. Such improvements yielded a slimmer receiver and a sharper focus of the electronic beam. However, a 90-degree deflection tube is most commonly used today in order to save electricity and reduce the price. In Japan, much greater emphasis is placed on these objectives, as well as improvement of quality.

Incorporation of solid-state technology provided many benefits, such as miniaturization, energy savings, higher reliability, and a quick-start image. Even the black-and-white television receivers of the early 1960s were able to realize these benefits with the successful application of solid-state technology. In addition, a new market for battery-charged portable sets was opened in the mid-1960s. However, it was with color television, using nearly three times as many parts as black-and-white, that the benefits of solid-state technology were the largest. Full transistorization of color television was achieved in 1969, and nearly all of the color receivers were changed to full transistor type the next year. The use of transistors decreased set size substantially, but the most appealing features to consumers were energy savings and a quick-start image. Hitachi led the Japanese companies in incorporating solid-state technology in its receivers and thereby increased its domestic market share. In this adoption process, the Japanese companies were quicker and much more adept than the Americans, and from this point on, they assumed a technological lead over the U.S. industry.

The next technological development to come along was the development of the integrated circuits, which has a profound impact on the color television industry in further reducing the cost of manufacturing by reducing the number of components needed. In addition, the integrated circuits were exactly what was needed to pursue the Japanese goal of further reducing power consumption of the sets, especially with the oil shortages of the 1970s. Considerable improvements were again made in developing low-power dissipation technology.

With the advent of integrated circuits, the goal of low-cost design was pursued with considerable success. This was especially necessary following the 1973 oil embargo when the Japanese color television industry faced a critical situation; materials, parts, and labor costs skyrocketed, while the market for finished sets softened appreciably, slowing economic recovery. Makers of television sets responded on three fronts: reduced part counts, automated production, and improved quality. Not only were the number of components greatly reduced, but with twenty years of component manufacturing experience behind them, the makers were also able to automate the assembly process itself by using the automatic insertion machine for parts and thereby reducing manual labor. Through this period, the average factory price declined consistently while the quality continued to improve. And most important, the competitive strength of the Japanese color television industry in the world market strengthened considerably.

The present trend in television R&D is toward a systems concept of home entertainment and use, and there are many new developments in industrial applications of the same television technology. Much attention is being paid to the new role that television receivers might play with the coming of cable television, mini-computers, and TV add-on equipment. The television receiver is moving toward becoming a display terminal for multipurpose use. TV add-on equipment such as video games, home VTR, educational equipment, and home computers promises to expand the traditional television industry much further in the consumer sector.

Appendix B:
Videotape Recorder
Technology

The videotape recorder (VTR) is probably the most significant new consumer electronics product available. The VTR was first developed in the United States by the Ampex Corporation in 1956 for broadcasts and was called the Quadruplex VTR. It was the Sony Corporation, however, that was able to take Ampex's $100,000 commercial model and develop a $10,000 consumer prototype and then redesign and reengineer a $1,000 mass-produced product. The actual production cost of the consumer VTR today is around $300. Sony's Betamax, Matsushita's VHS format, and Quasar's VR 1000 are the three major VTRs on the market today.

To record and recover the high frequencies needed to produce a moving color television image from a cassette tape is not simple. The performance of all magnetic recording systems is limited primarily by the minimum practical recording wavelength at a given signal frequency and tape speed. Since Ampex's introduction of the commercial VTR, reduction in minimum recording wavelength, video head track width, and tape area consumption per hour have allowed home VTR products to emerge.

The video recorder, which weighs about forty pounds and hooks up to all makes and models of television sets, is extremely versatile. In addition to recording on-air programs while the viewer may be watching another channel, it can record programs automatically with the aid of a timer. The viewer can also purchase and play prerecorded tapes of movies and television shows, both authorized and pirated. The manufacturers offer an optional camera to make home movies that can be viewed on the television set.

The manufacture of components and accessories (tapes), in terms of sophistication of manufacturing techniques and particularly precision of manufacture and quality control standards, represents a quantum jump beyond color television technology. For this reason the technical advances in product design and production engineering by Japanese manufacturers have been critical to the commercial lead that Japanese industry has taken in this area.

Selected Bibliography

Chapter 1

Abelson, Philip H., and Hammond, Allen L., ed. *Electronics: The Continuing Revolution.* Washington, D.C.: American Association for the Advancement of Science, 1977.

Charles River Associates Inc. *International Technological Competitiveness: Television Receivers and Semiconductors.* Boston, Mass.: Charles River Associates, Inc. July 1979.

Patrick, Hugh, and Rosovsky, Henry, ed. *Asia's New Giant: How the Japanese Economy Works.* Washington, D.C.: Brookings Institution, 1976.

Sato, Kazuo. "The Japanese Economy at the Crossroads." Paper presented at the Columbia University Seminar on Modern East Asia, April 11, 1980.

Tsurumi, Yoshi. *The Japanese Are Coming.* Cambridge, Mass.: Ballinger Publishing Co., 1976.

Yoshino, M.Y. *Japan's Multinational Enterprises.* Cambridge, Mass.: Harvard University Press, 1976.

Chapter 2

Denison, Edward F., and William K. Chung. *How Japan's Economy Grew So Fast: The Sources of Postwar Expansion.* Washington, D.C.: Brookings Institution, 1976.

Ikeda, Masayoshi. "Subcontracting System in the Japanese Electronics Industry." *Engineering Industries of Japan* (May 1979).

"Japan (III): Industrial Research Struggles to Close the Gap." *Science,* January 16, 1970.

Kaplan, Eugene J. *Japan: The Government-Business Relationship.* Washington, D.C.: U.S. Department of Commerce, February 1972.

Mason, R. Hal. "Japanese Technology Transfer Practices: A Comparative Examination." Unpublished report. 1979.

Saxonhouse, Gray R. "Industrial Restructuring in Japan." *Journal of Japanese Studies* 5, no. 2 (1979).

UNESCO. *Technological Development in Japan.* Paris: UNESCO, 1971.

Chapter 3

Dempa Publication, Inc. *Japan Fact Book 1979: A Comprehensive Guide to Japan's Electronics Industry and Manufacturers.* Tokyo: Dempa Publication, Inc., 1979.

Electronics Association of Japan. *Electronics in Japan, 1968-1979.* Tokyo: Electronics Association of Japan, 1980.

"From Survival and Revival to Evolution and Devolution." *Journal of the Electronics Industry* (November 1979).

"Japan's Matsushita, Once a Copycat, Claws Way to the Top with Innovative Technology." *Wall Street Journal,* November 21, 1979.

Nikko Securities Co., Ltd. *Current Situation of Video Tape Recorders, Related Products, Parts and Components.* Tokyo: Nikko Securities, Ltd., September 19, 1977.

Pearlstine, Norman. "That Old Nobushi Spirit." *Forbes,* July 23, 1979.

Sugata, Eizi, and Namekawa, Toshihiko. "Integrated Circuits for Television Receivers." *IEEE Spectrum* (May 1979).

"What Makes Japan's Electronics Different?" *Journal of the Electronics Industry* (August 1979).

Chapter 4

Callahan, Caryl A. *Business-Government Relations in Japan.* Los Angeles: Pacific Basin Economic Study Center at University of California, 1980.

Hirono, Ryokichi. *National Report—Japan: Factors Which Hinder or Help Productivity Improvement in the Asian Region.* Tokyo: Asia Productivity Organization Basic Research Project, 1979.

The Plan for Information Society: A National Goal Toward Year 2000. Tokyo: Japan Computer Usage Development Institute. May 1972.

Japan External Trade Organization. *White Paper on International Trade: Japan 1979.* Tokyo: Japan External Trade Organization, 1979.

"Japan's Gentle Persuaders." *Economist,* January 17, 1981.

Massachusetts Institute of Technology/Center for Policy Alternatives. *National Support for Science and Technology: An Examination of the Foreign Experience.* 2 vols., Cambridge, Mass.: MIT/CPA, August 18, 1975.

Ministry of International Trade and Industry. *Japan's Industrial Structure—A Long Range Vision, 1978 Edition.* Tokyo: MITI, 1978.

Nippon Hoso Kyokai, *A Profile of NHK.* Tokyo: NHK, 1977.

_____ . *Broadcasting in Japan: An Historical Review.* Tokyo: NHK, 1963.

_____ . *50 Years of Japanese Broadcasting.* Tokyo: NHK, 1977.

_____ . NHK Lab Report. (1965-1979.)

The Machinery Temporary Measures Act. Tokyo: Japanese Government. 1956.

The Provisional Measures Law for the Promotion of the Specified Electronic and Machine Industry. Tokyo: Japanese Government. 1957.

The Provisional Measures Law for the Promotion of the Electronic Industry. Tokyo: Japanese Government. 1971.

The Provisional Measures Law for the Promotion of the Specific Machinery and Information Industry. Tokyo: Japanese Government. 1978.

Chapter 5

"A Shift in Priority from Exporting to Production Abroad: Sony's Overseas Sales Strategy." *Business Community Quarterly of Japan* (Autumn 1979).

"Asian Plans to Manufacture in U.S. Sharpens Color TV's Competitive Picture." *Retailing Home Furnishings,* August 20, 1979.

Department of State. *The Great Japanese Factory Controversy—The American Box Score, 1977-78.* Washington, D.C.: Government Printing Office, 1978.

"Japanese Electronics and Electrical Manufacturing Companies: Gradual Entry into the U.S. Industrial Market." *Economic World* (September 1979).

Kraar, Louis. "Japan's Canon Focuses on America." *Fortune,* January 12, 1981.

Ogawa, Masamichi. *Local Production of Color TV in the U.S. and Its Impacts on Related Industries.* Research Report. Tokyo: Small Business Finance Corp., 1979. (Translated from Japanese.)

Tsurumi, Yoshi. "The Strategic Framework for Japanese Investments in the U.S." *Columbia Journal of World Business* (December 1973).

Chapter 6

"American Manufacturers Strive for Quality—Japanese Style." *Business Week,* March 12, 1979.

Arthur D. Little Co. *Trends in the U.S. Marketplace for Color Television Sets.* Cambridge, Mass.: Arthur D. Little, 1980.

Center for the Interdisciplinary Study of Science and Technology. Northwestern University. *The U.S. Consumer Electronics Industry and Foreign Competition: An Analysis.* Evanstown, Ill.: Northwestern University. March 1980.

Nevin, John. "Can the Species Be Saved?" *Appliance Manufacturer* (February 1977).

"The Mess in Consumer Electronics." *Dun's Review* (June 1977).

Thomas H. Miner and Associates, Inc. *A Market Entry Study of Japan for Zenith Sales Corporation.* Chicago, Ill.: Thomas M. Miner and Associates, Inc. March 19, 1970.

U.S.-Japan Trade Council. *U.S.-Japan Competition in Semiconductors.* Part 1, December 7, 1979; Part 2, January 2, 1980; Part 3, March 7, 1980. Washington, D.C.; U.S.-Japan Trade Council.

Chapter 7

Booz, Allen and Hamilton, Inc. *Opportunities for the U.S. Consumer Electronics Industry.* Cleveland, Ohio: Booz, Allen and Hamilton, Inc. October 12, 1979.

Hayes, Robert H., and Abernathy, William J. "Managing Our Way to Economic Decline." *Harvard Business Review* (July-August 1980).

Juran, J.M. "Japanese and Western Quality—A Contrast." *Management Review* (November 1978).

Samuelson, Robert J. "U.S., Japan Find Old Relationships Have Unraveled." *National Journal,* June 30, 1979.

Sciberras, Edmund. *International Competitiveness and Technical Change: A Study of the U.S. Consumer Electronics Industry.* University of Sussex Science Policy Research Unit, September 25, 1979.

Zysman, John; Tyson, Laura; and Millstein, James E. "The Politics of Industrial Development and Trade Adjustment: A Case Study of the U.S. Television Receiver Industry." Unpublished paper. August 1979.

Chapter 8

B.A. Asia Limited. *The Japanese Semiconductor Industry: An Overview.* Hong Kong: B.A. Asia, Ltd., January 1979.

Holden, Constance. "Innovation: Japan Races Ahead as U.S. Falters." *Science,* November 14, 1980.

"Japan Goal: Lead in Computers." *New York Times,* December 12, 1979.

"Japan Moves Fast to Tackle Rapid Industrial Changes." *Journal of the Electronics Industry* (August 1979).

Kawase, Takeshi, and Rubenstein, Albert H. "Reactions of Japanese Industrial Managers to Incentive to Innovate—An Empirical Study."

IEEE Transactions on Engineering Management EM-24, no. 3 (August 1977).

"The Buying Consumer: Tracing the Patterns—Color Television." *Appliance Manufacturer*. (October 1979).

Torrero, Edward A. "Electro-Technology in Japan Today." *IEEE Spectrum* (September 1977).

"VCRs: Clarifying the Picture of their Worldwide Prospects." *Journal of the Electronics Industry* (March 1979).

Chapter 9

Chang, Y.S. "The Analysis of the Offshore Activities of the Japanese Electronics Industry." Unpublished report. November 1972.

Department of State. Bureau of Intelligence and Research. *Japanese Overseas Investment*. Report no. 475. June 1, 1976.

"Diversify and Expand: Matsushita's Production Strategy for North America." *Economic World* (August 1979).

Techno Systems Corporation. *Japanese Videoplayers Strategies and Its Impacts on the World Market*. Tokyo: Techno Systems Corporation. July 1977.

Chapter 10

Abernathy, William J. *The Productivity Dilemma: Roadblock to Innovation in the Automobile Industry*. Baltimore: Johns Hopkins University Press, 1978.

Chang, Chan Sup. "The Japanese Motor Vehicle Industry: A Study of the History of the Industry and the Impact of Japanese Motor Vehicles on the U.S. Market." Ph.D. dissertation, American University, 1974.

Kuroiwa, Toshiro. "Japan's Automobile Industry Technology." *The Wheel Extended* (September 1977).

Muto, Hiromichi, and Uneo, Hiroya. "The Automobile Industry of Japan." *Japan Economic Studies* (Fall 1974).

Nikko Research Center, Ltd. *Japan's Automobile Industry—Toyota Motor and Nissan Motor*. Tokyo: Nikko, 1977.

Sekaly, R.R. *Transnationalization of the Automotive Industry*. Ottawa: Institute for International Co-operation, 1979.

Weiers, Bruce, and Byron, George, ed. *Automotive Manufacturers Profiles of Japanese Automotive Industry*. Prepared by the Transportation

Systems Center for the National Highway Traffic Safety Administration, May 1978.

Supplemental Bibliography

Books

Boston Consulting Group. *Pacific Partnership: U.S.-Japan.* Lexington, Mass.: Japan Society, Inc. 1977.
Dempa Publications, Inc. *Japan Fact Book 1980.* Tokyo, 1980.
OECD. *The Industrial Policy of Japan.* Paris, 1972.
Tsurumi, Yoshi. *Japanese Business: A Research Guide with Annotated Bibliography.* New York: Praeger, 1978.

Government Documents

Japanese (in English)

Economic Planning Agency. *Economic Survey of Japan.* 1977-1978.
Japan External Trade Organization. *White Paper on International Trade: Japan 1979.*
MITI. *News from MITI.*
NHK. *Broadcast Engineering of NHK.* 1965-1979.
_____ . This Is NHK. 1965-1970.

United States

Comptroller General of the U.S. *U.S.-Japan Trade: Issues and Problems.* September 21, 1979.
Department of Commerce. *News.*
Department of Labor. Bureau of Labor Statistics and Office of Productivity and Technology. *Estimated Hourly Compensation of Production Workers in Specified Industries Related to Color Television Receiving Equipment Manufacturing in the United States, Mexico, Japan, Korea and Taiwan, 1975-1978.* April 1979.
_____ . *Profile of Labor in the Radio and Television Receiving Sets Industry.* May 1974.
International Trade Commission. *Television Receivers, Color and Monochrome, Assembled or Not Assembled, Finished or Not Finished, and Subassemblies Thereof.* Publication 808, Washington, D.C., March 1977.

_____ . OMA Pre-hearing Statements. March 5, 1980: Ivars Gutmanis, on behalf of the Electronics Industries Association of Japan; Stanley Nehmer, on behalf of COMPACT; M. Tanaka, on behalf of the Electronic Industries Association of Japan; Samuel L. Young, on behalf of the Electronic Industries Association of Korea.

Statement of John Nevin before House Subcommittee on Trade. September 21, 1978.

Reports

Aron, Paul. *Robotics in Japan: Paul Aron Reports No. 22.* New York: Daiwa Securities America, Inc., July 3, 1980.

Electronics Industries Association of Japan. *Electronics Industries in Japan.* Tokyo 1976-1979.

Japan Electronics Industry Development Association. *Guide to JEIDA.* Tokyo. 1979-1980.

_____ . *Electronic Industries in Japan.* Tokyo. 1979-1980.

Morgan, Stanley. *Progress Report on Hitachi.* New York. March 7, 1980.

National Academy of Engineering. *Industrial Innovation and Public Policy Options: Report of a Colloquium.* Washington, D.C.: National Academy Press, 1980.

Tsurumi, Yoshi, and Tsurumi, Hiroki. *A Bayesian Test of the Product Life Cycle Hypothesis as Applied to the U.S. Demand for Color TV Sets.* Los Angeles: University of California Pacific Basin Economic Study Center, Working Paper Series, No. 1, September 1978.

Wheatley, John J., and Oshikawa, Sadaomi. "Marketing in Japan: Problems and Possibilities for American Business." Unpublished report. 1974.

U.S.-Japan Trade Council. *Japanese Import Licensing Procedure.* Fact Sheet No. 8. August 20, 1971.

Japanese Television Exports to the U.S.: An Update. Council Report No. 32. July 25, 1978.

Speeches

Arai, Joji, Japan Productivity Center. To Monterrey Productivity Center, Monterrey, Mexico. February 13, 1980.

Index

Index

AEG Telefunken, 40, 138
Aichi Steel Works, 159
Alps Electric Co., 33
Ampex Corporation, 39, 171
Arab states, consumer electronics market in, 142
Ashai Glass Company, 33
Asia, consumer electronics market in, 140
audio-equipment industry, U.S., offshore manufacture in, 101
audio-video synthetic system, 133
audiovisual communications system, 135
automatic insertion machine, 170
automobile industry, Japan, 13: comparison to consumer electronics industry, 147; corporate goals of, 154; corporate structure of, 157; exports of, 149, 157-158; foreign operations of, 19, 158-159; government role in, 19-20, 152, 153, 156-157; historical development of, 150-154; major firms of, 148; markets for, 148-149; production process in, 154-156; production rate of, 147-148; technology transfers in, 152-153
automobile industry, U.S.: in Japanese market, 149; production process in, 156; vertical integration of, 159-160
Automobile Manufacturing Enterprise Law (1936), 151

Bank of Japan, 11, 20, 70-71, 151
banks, Japan: interest rates of, 11; loan policies of, 27, 70, 157
Betamax videotape recorder, 43, 45, 102
Brazil, Japanese subsidiaries in, 141
Britain: Japanese imports to, 139; Japanese subsidiaries in, 138-139
business-copier market, 6

cable television, two-way, interactive, 135-136
Canada, consumer electronics market in, 142
Canon Company, 164
cathode-ray tubes, color, Japanese production of, 33
CBS laboratories, 37
China, consumer electronics market in, 141-142
Chrysler Corporation, 19, 156
citizen-band (CB) radio, 36
color television technology, 23, 50, 52; on chassis, 44; early developments in, 37; in export market adaptations, 119-120; importation of, 38; integrated circuits in, 170; for large-size screen, 44, 45, 90; multiplex receivers in, 134; picture tube in, 169; remote-control devices in, 90; satellite-to-home, 134; solid-state, 106-107, 169-170; trends in, 170; voice-synthesis systems in, 128, 132, 133. *See also* research and development (R&D)
Committee for the Preservation of American Color Television (COMPACT), 82, 99
computer, home, 136
computer equipment industry, 56
consumer electronics industry, Japan: comparison to automobile industry, 147; competitive strengths of, 4, 125-126; domestic market of, 34; export incentives to, 70-71; export price system of, 67-68; foreign competition and, 34; future of, 126-127; government assistance to, 55-57, 69-70; government market development for, 61-63; government protection of, 63-68; government research for, 59-63, 128; high-technology componentry of, 131-132; horizontal product spread in, 90, 132-133;

About the Author

Jack Baranson is president and research director of Developing World Industry and Technology, Inc., a policy research and consulting group. Recent studies he has directed include *Commercial Consequences of Technology Sharing under NATO Arms Collaboration Agreements* (for the U.S. Department of Defense) and *The Technology Factor in U.S. Trade Policy* (for the U.S. Special Trade Representative's Office). He has been a consultant to industry, foreign governments, and international agencies on the technology factor in world trade, investment, and development.

Dr. Baranson was a visiting lecturer at the Harvard Business School in 1972 and served for six years as a staff economist at the World Bank (1965-1971). Previously he has served as a research associate with the Brookings Institution, the Committee for Economic Development, and the International Development Research Center at Indiana University. Dr. Baranson received the doctoral degree in economics from Indiana University and the master's degree from the Johns Hopkins School of Advanced International Studies. He is the author of *Automotive Industries in Developing Countries* and *Technology and the Multinationals: Corporate Strategies in a Changing World Economy.*